CONTENTS

Introduction

Religions and Beliefs in Britain is the ninety-fourth volume in the **Issues** series. The aim of this series is to offer up-to-date information about important issues in our world.

Religions and Beliefs in Britain looks at religious diversity and tolerance in Britain.

The information comes from a wide variety of sources and includes:
Government reports and statistics
Newspaper reports and features
Magazine articles and surveys
Website material
Literature from lobby groups
and charitable organisations.

It is hoped that, as you read about the many aspects of the issues explored in this book, you will critically evaluate the information presented. It is important that you decide whether you are being presented with facts or opinions. Does the writer give a biased or an unbiased report? If an opinion is being expressed, do you agree with the writer?

Religions and Beliefs in Britain offers a useful starting-point for those who need convenient access to information about the many issues involved. However, it is only a starting-point. At the back of the book is a list of organisations which you may want to contact for further information.

*****

Guide to religions in the UK

Are you a Zoroastrian? What do Catholics, Sikhs and Hindus believe? Find out with our guide to the main religions practised in the UK today

Christianity and the Christian tradition

Anglicanism

The Anglican Communion is a loosely organised community of Protestant churches, whose 'mother church' is the Church of England, established by the Act of Supremacy in 1534 (during the English Reformation). Others include the Church in Wales, the Scottish Episcopal Church, and the Church of Ireland.

Baptists

Baptists hold six convictions in common: supreme authority of the Bible; baptism of believers only; a church comprised of believers only; equal status of all Christians within the church; independence of local churches; and separation of church and state.

Charismatic Renewal

Founded by US Catholics in 1967, the Charismatic Renewal movement seeks a return to traditional teaching and values, while emphasising the spiritual rebirth of believers.

Church of Jesus Christ of Latter-Day Saints (Mormons)

Founded in 1830s America by Joseph Smith, who revealed the Book of Mormon, telling of Israelite migration to America centuries before Christ. Adherents are millennialist, believing a second coming of Jesus Christ will be followed by 1,000 years of peace under his rule.

Church of Scotland

State church of Scotland, founded in 1560 along Calvinist principles. In 1690 it developed a Presbyterian form of governance – a collective including both clergy and non-clerical elders. The church has no set prayer-book or order of service; communion is generally celebrated only occasionally.

Jehovah's Witnesses

Millennialist faith, founded by Charles Taze Russell in 1870-80. Believers reject the Trinity, saying Jesus is the son of Jehovah but not an embodiment of God. They are active evangelists.

Methodism

Founded in 1739 by John Wesley, who wanted to emphasise the power of the Holy Spirit in the faith and personal life of believers, and the value of a personal relationship with God.

Orthodoxy

The Orthodox church split from Catholicism in the 'great schism' of 1054, over papal supremacy and aspects of the nature of God. The church in the UK now represents a combination of jurisdictions, primarily the ecumenical patriarchate, but also Greek, Russian, Serbian and Antiochian traditions.

Pentecostalism

Pentecostal beliefs have their roots in Protestantism. Members are baptised into the spirit, availing them to the spiritual gifts of God which may include speaking in tongues, and the ability to prophesy and heal.

Quakers (Religious Society of Friends)

Quakerism was founded by George Fox during the 17th-century English Puritan movement. Believing that there is something of God in everyone, Quakers reject barriers of race, sex or creed. Meetings of worship are characterised by silence, during which anyone may feel moved to speak, pray or read.

Roman Catholicism

Church dating back to the Apostles of Jesus Christ in the 1st century AD. Unlike Protestants, Roman Catholics believe in the literal transformation of bread and wine into the body and blood of Christ (also known as transubstantiation). Unlike the Orthodox, they believe in the 'supreme jurisdiction' of the Pope – one of the issues that led to the 'great schism' of Catholicism and Orthodoxy in 1054.

Salvation Army

Christian religious and charity movement founded by William Booth, a London Methodist minister, in 1865. Doctrinally similar to most Protestant evangelical denominations. Services are informal.

Seventh-Day Adventist Church

Millennial faith, established in the US largely through the preaching of William Miller (1782-1849). Adherents share many basic Christian beliefs. Principles include the observation of the seventh day of the week rather than the first as the Sabbath.

Unitarianism

Form of Christianity that rejects the concept of the Trinity, believing instead in the oneness of God. Also believe in the 'essential unity of humankind and of creation', espousing a liberal, tolerant attitude to other branches of faith.

United Reformed Church

Formed in 1972 with the union of the Congregational Church in England and Wales and the Presbyterian Church of England.

Other religions

Baha'i

Founded in Iran in 1844, principally by Mirza Hoseyn Ali Nuri – or Baha Ullah (Glory of God). He and his forerunner, Mirza Ali Muhammad (the Bab), are held to be manifestations of God, who in his essence is unknowable. The Baha'i seek to establish a universal faith, and are devoted to abolition of racial, class and religious prejudices.

Buddhism

Religion and philosophy founded by Siddhartha Guatama (Buddha), possibly in the 5th century BC. According to his Four Noble Truths, the human condition is one of suffering caused by the craving for temporary things. One of these espouses a search for enlightenment and nirvana – a deliverance from human existence.

Hinduism

Both a civilisation and a congregation of religions, having neither a founder, central authority, hierarchy nor organisation. Most sects accept the sacredness of the ancient Indian Veda texts of 1400 to 500 BC. Hindus believe in reincarnation, the worship of several gods, and a caste system as the basis of society.

Islam

The sources of Islam are the Koran, believed by Muslims to be the exact word of God, and the Hadith – the report of the sayings, deeds and approvals of the Prophet Muhammad. Tenets include the oneness of God, the equality of mankind, the innocence of man at birth, and the inseparability of religion and politics. Has two principal branches: Sunni and Shia.

Jainism

Although precise origins are unknown, most believers come from the Gujarat and Rajasthan areas of India. Jains are followers of the Jinas or Tirthankaras (spiritual victors) – an ancient line of teachers said to possess infinite knowledge and to have attained perfect purity. The principal belief is ahimsa – the avoidance, where possible, of physical or mental harm to any living being.

Judaism

Jews believe they are the descendants of Abraham, who received a covenant from God around 2000 BC. This covenant was enhanced 500 years later by the Torah, five books given by God to Moses on Mount Sinai. Jews believe that they are challenged and blessed by God, who compels them to obey his laws and act as witness for other peoples of the world.

Paganism

Paganism encompasses several spiritual movements, many of which predate the major religions. Based on the ancient polytheistic religions of Europe and the Middle East, the focus is a spirituality linked to the cyclical and rhythmic patterns of nature.

Rastafarian

Rastafarians worship Haile Selassie I (known as Ras [Prince] Tafari), former emperor of Ethiopia, considering him to have been the Messiah and champion of the black race. Rastas believe black people are Israelites reincarnated and have been persecuted by the white race in divine punishment for their sins. They will eventually be redeemed by exodus to Africa, their true home and heaven on earth.

Scientology

Religious/scientific movement spawned by dianetics, a programme developed by the American L. Ron Hubbard in the 1950s. According to dianetics, every experience is recorded in the mind as a mental image: it espouses a set of techniques, including working with an 'auditor', to free the mind of latent painful memories or 'engrams'.

Sikhism
Indian religion combining Islamic and Hindu elements, founded in the Punjab in the late 15th century by Guru Nanak. Nanak was the first of

the Ten Gurus, of whom Sikhs are disciples. There is one God, whom man should serve by leading a life of prayer and obedience: Sikhs believe

that their soul then passes through various existences by transmigration, and will become one with God.

Zoroastrians
Religion founded between 6000 and 12000 BC in north-east Iran. Scriptures describe the will of Ahura Mazda (Lord of Wisdom), the all-powerful and perfect creator, who grants humans Vohu Manah – a clear, rational mind with which to dispel ignorance and blind faith.

© Guardian Newspapers Limited 2004

Religions

A history of diversity

The UK has greater religious diversity than any other country in the European Union. This is a direct result of historical immigration patterns, particularly times when people from Commonwealth countries were encouraged to enter the country to fill labour shortages.

The numbers
It is difficult to compare membership numbers for religious groups as different communities gather figures in different ways and labels don't always fit. Religious and ethnic groups also tend to get confused or overlap – Sikhs and Jews, for example, can be categorised as belonging to ethnic groups as much as religious ones.

A distinction is also made between active and passive religious affiliation. In 1994, for example, the total number of people alive who had been baptised into the Church of England was 26.2m but the membership roll of the church numbered just over 1.76m, with fewer than 1m actually attending church.

The six largest religious groups
Based on the 2001 Census figures for England and Wales the two countries are made up of . . .
- 37,338,486 Christians
- 1,546,626 Muslims
- 552,421 Hindus
- 329,358 Sikhs

- 259,927 Jews
- 144,453 Buddhists.
  The census also identified . . .
- 150,720 people who claimed a religion other than the ones above
- 7,709,267 who claimed to have no religion
- 4,010,658 who declined to state a religion.

The numbers in Northern Ireland
In Northern Ireland 43.76 per cent of people identified themselves as Catholic, 53.13 per cent as Protestant or other Christian, 0.39 per cent as

Buddhist Temple

belonging to another religion and 2.725 per cent as having no religion.

Religious festivals
Beliefs, holy days, feasts, fasts and celebrations
Within each of the major world religions there are many different groups and variations. Not all members of a given religion will celebrate all of that religion's festivals but here is a list of important occasions for each . . .

Christians
The Christian Church is made up of people who worship God through Jesus. They believe that God became a human being in the form of Jesus.

The festivals of the Christian Church mainly relate to the life of Jesus and the Christian saints. The most important are . . .
- Christmas – the birth of Jesus
- Good Friday – the death of Jesus on the cross
- Easter – the resurrection of Jesus from the dead
- Ascension – the return of Jesus into heaven
- Pentecost – the coming of the Holy Spirit and the birth of the Church.

Muslims
The five pillars of Islam are to . . .
- worship the one God, Allah
- pray five times a day
- give alms

- fast
- go to Mecca on pilgrimage at least once.

Islam means 'submission' (understood as 'submission to the will of God'). Islamic festivals commemorate the submission of the Prophet Muhammad and other prophets to the will of Allah.

The main festivals of the Muslim year are . . .
- Ramadan – the month of fasting
- Al Hijrah – Muslim New Year
- Eid-Ul-Milad – birthday of the Prophet Muhammad
- Lailut-Ul-Isra – the night of the journey and ascension
- Lailut-Ul-Barah – the night of forgiveness
- Eid-Ul-Adha – the festival of sacrifice
- Eid Ul-Fitr – the end of Ramadan.

Hindus

Hindus believe there is one supreme eternal God, who is formless, beyond space, time and human comprehension. There are about 330 million representations of the one supreme God. The Hindu trinity is the most powerful of the manifestations and consists of Lord Brahma (the Creator of the Universe), Lord Vishnu (the Preserver of the Universe) and Lord Shiva (the Destroyer of the Universe).

Hindus follow their religion in a great variety of ways and hold a wide assortment of festivals. The following are the better-known ones in the UK . . .
- Shivaratri – dedicated to Lord Shiva
- Holi – the welcoming of spring

- Rama Navami – birthday of Lord Rama
- Janamashtami – birthday of Lord Krishna
- Navaratri – festival of nine lights dedicated to the three main Goddesses of Hinduism (Parvati, Lakshmi & Sarasvati)
- Diwali – festival of light
- Annakuta – Hindu New Year.

Sikhs

The Sikhs ('disciples') are followers of the 15th- and 16th-century Guru, Nanak. Sikhs seek spiritual harmony through individual meditation upon Waheguru (God).

The Sikh panth – or community – is open to all, regardless of caste, sex or previous misdeeds.

Important Sikh festivals include . . .
- the Gurpurbs festivals – commemorating events in the life of Sikh spiritual leaders or gurus, including the birthday of Guru Nanak and the birthday of Guru Gobind Singh
- the martyrdoms of Sri Guru Tigh Bahadur and of Guru Arjun Dev
- Baisakh – a harvest festival

- Hola Mohalla – an annual festival and parade.

Jews

Judaism was the first religion to believe in one God. It is based on belief and trust in God and in carrying out his rules for living – the Ten Commandments.

Jews worship in synagogues, where the traditional language of prayer is Hebrew, although English is also used in some services today.

Judaism celebrates many festivals, including . . .
- Rosh Hashanah – New Year
- Yom Kippur – the Day of Atonement
- Sukkot – harvest festival
- Chanukkah – Festival of Lights
- Pesach – Passover.

Buddhists

Buddhists believe that if they follow the teaching of the Lord Buddha, the founder of their faith, they can attain Nirvana, a state of bliss.

Buddhist festivals are linked to the Buddha's life and teaching – the main ones are . . .
- Omisoka – New Year
- Buddha Purnima – birthday of the Buddha
- Vesak Puja – enlightenment of the Buddha
- Purinirvana – death of the Buddha
- Poson – introduction of Buddhism to Sri Lanka
- Dhammacakka/Asala – the turning of the Wheel of Truth

- The above information is excerpted from Common Purpose's website: www.commonpurpose.org.uk

© Common Purpose 2004

WHAT WOULD HAPPEN IF ALL THE RELIGIONS GOT TOGETHER?

-LIFE WOULD BE ONE LONG FESTIVAL!

Census proves the force of Christianity

Most people in England and Wales – 71.1 per cent – still regard themselves as Christians, the first official count of religious affiliation has found.

Despite the sharp decline in churchgoing and the growth of secularism, 37.3 million described their religion as Christianity, according to the 2001 Census published February 2003.

The census, the first to ask a question on religion, confirmed Islam as the second largest faith, with 1.54 million (3.1 per cent).

It also recorded 552,000 Hindus (1.1 per cent), 329,000 Sikhs (0.6 per cent), 260,000 Jews (0.5), 144,000 Buddhists (0.3) and 150,000 (0.3) from other religions.

Just over four million refused to answer the question, which was voluntary, and 7.7 million (14.8) said they had no religion.

Though most of the figures were broadly in line with previous estimates, the census produced some surprises.

The North East emerged as the most Christian region of the country, although it has one of the lowest rates of church attendance. The North West districts of St Helens, Wigan and Copeland had the highest proportions of Christians (86 per cent or more).

Even more unexpectedly Norwich in Norfolk, which once boasted having one church for every week of the year, was the least devout place, recording the highest proportion of people of no religion (27.8 per cent). It was followed by Brighton and Hove, and Cambridge.

The Bishop of Norwich, the Rt Rev Graham James, said: 'Norwich has a higher than average level of church attendance. So, if it is the least religious place in the country, it has an odd way of showing it.

'Plainly there is still plenty of scope for further mission but I suspect that what affects the

By Jonathan Petre,
Religion Correspondent

statistics is that Norwich, unlike many cities, has only a very small representation of other faiths.'

> **Despite the sharp decline in churchgoing and the growth of secularism, 37.3 million described their religion as Christianity, according to the 2001 Census**

Brighton also surfaced as the spiritual home of an unlikely movement which can now claim more adherents than the Sikhs, Jews or Buddhists – the Jedi Knights.

Star Wars devotees were encouraged by an internet campaign to register themselves as Jedi, intergalactic warriors able to harness a mysterious energy field called the Force, under the misapprehension that, if more than 10,000 did, it would be recognised as an official religion.

Despite the efforts of census officials to counter the campaign, 390,000 people (0.7 per cent), mostly in university towns, gave their religion as Jedi.

Len Cook, the Registrar General for England and Wales, said they had been categorised

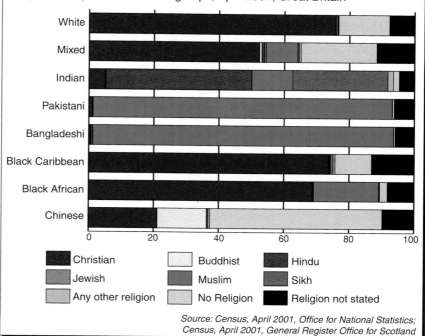

Ethnicity and identity

The 2001 Census collected information about ethnicity and religious identity. Combining these results shows that while the population of Great Britain is more culturally diverse than ever before, White Christians remain the largest single group by far. In Great Britain, 36 million people (nearly 7 out of 10) described their ethnicity as White and their religion as Christian.

Religious composition of ethnic groups, April 2001, Great Britain

Legend: Christian, Buddhist, Hindu, Jewish, Muslim, Sikh, Any other religion, No Religion, Religion not stated

Source: Census, April 2001, Office for National Statistics; Census, April 2001, General Register Office for Scotland

among those who said they had no religion.

'I suspect this was a decision which will not be challenged greatly,' he said. 'I think there are other reasons why something should be classed as a religion, rather than a group of people getting together on the internet.'

The highest proportion of Muslims, Hindus, Buddhists and Jews is in London, with 36.4 per cent of the borough of Tower Hamlets describing themselves as Muslim. However Sikhs are most highly concentrated in Slough.

Despite the number calling themselves Christian, only about 11 per cent now go to church at least once a month.

The Bishop of Lichfield, the Rt Rev Keith Sutton, said: 'These figures prove as a lie the claims by the National Secular Society and others that England is no longer a Christian country.

'But welcome as they are, they are a wake-up call to Christian leadership. While the Christian faith remains relevant to the majority of society, the Church is clearly no longer seen as important.'

© Telegraph Group Limited, London 2004

Turning from God

Young people and religion

Statistics suggest that fewer and fewer young people now bother to attend church. Has religion become an irrelevance to modern British teenagers? A team of Children's Express reporters interviewed other young people to find out

For some people, religion is everything. 'We sacrifice our life for religion, because we are so into it,' says Imran, a 15-year-old Muslim from Sheffield. 'And we want to pass that on to our generation.'

He continues: 'We came down here on this Earth to believe in God, to spread Islam around the world. That's what our prophet did. He used to go everywhere, anywhere, to spread Islam about, so that's what our job is.'

Esther, who is a Christian, agrees. 'You can talk to friends about your beliefs and stuff. I mean the whole thing is because you want to get your friends into church, you want to get your friends to become Christians. And if they can see it in you, they're more likely to change.'

These are not sentiments which you would normally associate with typical British teenagers – at least, not as characterised in the popular press. Yet neither Imran nor Esther is an extremist; they are just young people with a strong faith.

However, Imran and Esther belong to a shrinking minority. Two-thirds of 18- to 24-year-olds in the UK say they have no religious affiliation and only a tiny number of young people go to church. Esther points out that even though she goes to a Catholic school, few of her fellow students are actually Christians. 'It's not cool to be a Christian,' she admits.

Even in the Muslim community, which is growing steadily, some young men are abandoning their faith. 'We have a lot of Muslim people who are not reading their prayers,' says Imran. 'They are just Muslim in

Factbox

Two-thirds of UK 18- to 24-year-olds say they have no religious affiliation, compared to just a quarter of pensioners
(British Social Attitudes Survey, National Centre for Social Research, Nov 2000)

48 per cent of UK residents claim to belong to a religion, compared to 86 per cent in the United States and 92 per cent in Italy
(British Social Attitudes Survey)

Since 1960, there has been a significant increase in the numbers of Muslims, Sikhs, Hindus and Buddhists in the UK
(UK Christian Handbook – Religious Trends)

A University of Wales survey of 33,000 teenagers aged 13 to 15 in 2000, found 51% who were brought up as Anglicans had no belief in God, compared to 19% brought up in non-Christian faiths (including 8% of Muslims and 35% of young people brought up in the Jewish faith).

name. People who should call themselves Muslims are people who say their prayers, who follow the right path, who respect their elders.'

The statistics (see box) and Imran and Esther's comments appear to lend support to the view that, when compared to other western nations, the UK has an overwhelmingly secular culture. But is this really proof of a spiritual decline in youth culture, or a sign that young people are more willing to explore non-traditional ways of expressing spiritual feeling? Or is rejection of the church a rejection of faith?

Reverend Mike Breen, Rector of St Thomas' United Anglican and Baptist Church in Sheffield – the largest church in the north of England – admits that many young people are turned off going to church because they find it dull.

'It's boring,' he says. 'Honestly. That's the church's fault. I'm a vicar and I think that I'm part of the establishment that's made it dull and I'm taking responsibility for that, to try to reverse it.'

Part of the problem, he says, is the church's failure to 'sell' religion to young people in terms that they might understand. 'Being a Christian doesn't mean going to church once a week and working through a 16th-century prayer book, it's about life.'

And at St Thomas', they do seem to be bucking the general trend. More than 70 per cent of Rev Breen's congregation is under 35, and one in five is under 21. In two years of holding weekly events at the Roxy in Sheffield's city centre, he estimates that 3,000 people have come through the doors.

The secret of his success is to present the church experience in terms that are familiar to modern young people. Services at St Thomas' have more in common with club culture than with traditional worship – despite the hedonistic associations of clubland. In a sense, young people at St Thomas' are seeking a spiritual high.

'A leader of our church said to me that she went to a Gatecrasher club night about a year ago,' says Rev Breen, 'and it was the closest thing to St Thomas' she'd ever seen. It was like worship service. I thought that was interesting, because obviously people who go to Gatecrasher are looking for something more than just the music.

'There is a community theme. You go to Ibiza once a year or you go to the club once a week, but what we've got going is something that's there every day, community life every day, and I think that's one of the reasons why people are so into it.'

Rev Breen claims the growth in his congregation is part of a larger movement of young people turning away from the materialistic ethos of their parents' generation. He links it to radical youth movements – such as environmental pressure groups and the anti-capitalism movement – which seem to represent an emerging set of spiritual beliefs.

'I think a lot of the way the Bible is taught is outdated, but I can't imagine how anybody who knows how to translate what's in there into the modern culture can say that they're outdated, because they're about life. At the end of Matthew chapter seven it says, "Treat people the way you want people to treat you". That can't possibly be outdated, can it?'

Yet despite Rev Breen's argument that the ethics of religion continue to be relevant, the figures suggest that fewer young people are willing to embrace a religious life. In an age dominated by science and materialism, more young people are rejecting the most central tenet of all religions – belief in God.

Belief

Which, if any, of the things I am going to read out do you believe in?

	Yes	No	Don't know
God	60%	29%	11%
Life after death	47%	43%	10%
A soul	68%	27%	6%
Heaven	52%	40%	8%
Astrology	31%	66%	4%
Ghosts	38%	56%	6%
Telepathy	42%	51%	7%
Guardian angels	40%	56%	4%
Premonitions/ESP	54%	41%	6%
Fortune telling/tarot	13%	83%	4%
Deja-vu	57%	38%	5%
Out of body experience	32%	61%	7%
Reincarnation	23%	68%	9%
Hell	32%	62%	6%
Near-death experience	60%	34%	7%
Psychics/mediums	28%	66%	6%
Faith healers	24%	68%	8%
That dreams can predict the future	25%	69%	65%

Source: Three In Five 'Believe in God', 8-17 August 2003. MORI

A survey of 33,000 13- to 15-year-olds carried out by the University of Wales in 2000, found that 51 per cent of young people growing up in the Anglican faith claimed to be atheist. Just eight per cent of young Muslims adopted this stance.

Merlin Evans, 15, from Sheffield, says: 'I have atheist parents but I don't think that's had much of an effect. It's more my interest in science and the difficulty of believing in something which isn't backed up by proof, reason and logic.

'I feel that God is created in the minds of human beings to create a sense of assurance and comfort. I have no problem with people believing in religion or believing in God – in many ways it helps people – but I just feel that we've made so many scientific breakthroughs that the possibility of having a physical god is just unthinkable.'

The fanaticism that can accompany religion is also a big turn-off, according to Merlin. By contrast, she says, atheism is more open, less condemning. 'There's so many

---

Since 1960, there has been a significant increase in the numbers of Muslims, Sikhs, Hindus and Buddhists in the UK

---

illogical and condemning ideas in the Bible that I find it too difficult to agree with,' she says. 'Christian views have caused severe difficulties for feminism.'

Since September 11, we have been sharply reminded that we live in a multicultural society that is often divided by faith. For some young people, the bigotry and extremism have put them off religion. For others, the increased focus on faith has given them a chance to reconsider their own.

As Rachel Twort, 21 and a convert to Islam, puts it: 'I think it's organised religion that is in decline, not the basic, inner beliefs. I grew up in a fairly agnostic household, but I have always felt the need for religion in my life.'

Nevertheless, children and teenagers are still largely undecided. Merlin sums up what is probably the best way to look at religion. 'You should come to your own conclusions, based on all the evidence,' she says.

■ This article was produced by Tessa Robins, 16, Saarah Choudhury, 16, and Jenny Matthews, 16, all from Sheffield. Children's Express is a programme of learning through journalism for young people aged 8-18. www.childrens-express.org

■ The above information is from YoungMinds' website which can be found at www.youngminds.org.uk
© YoungMinds

Different faiths shared values

Information from the Inter Faith Network

The golden rule

Each faith has teachings about the importance of dealing rightly with other people. This principle – to treat others as we would wish to be treated ourselves – is sometimes called the 'Golden Rule'.

Bahá'i faith

Lay not on any soul a load which ye would not wish to be laid upon you, and desire not for any one the things ye would not desire for yourselves.

This is My best counsel unto you, did ye but ye observe it.

Baha'u'llah. Gleanings, 128

Buddhism

Just as a mother would protect her only child with her life, even so let one cultivate a boundless love towards all beings.

Khuddaka Patha, from the Metta Sutta

Christianity

Do to others as you would have them do to you.   Luke 6.31

Islam

No one of you is a believer until he desires for his brother that which he desires for himself.

An-Nawawi's Forty Hadith, 13

Jainism

I forgive all beings, may all beings forgive me, I have friendship towards all, malice towards none.

Pratikraman Sutra 35:49

Judaism

What is hateful to you, do not do to your fellow man.

Talmud: Shabbat 31a

Sikhism

No one is my enemy, and no one is a stranger. I get along with everyone.

Sri Guru Granth Sahib p. 1299

Hinduism

This is the sum of duty: do naught to others which if done to thee would cause thee pain.

Mahabharata 5.1517

Zoroastrianism

That nature only is good when it shall not do unto another whatever is not good for its own self.

Dadistan-I-Dinik 94.5

3 big myths

Big myth 1: Well, they may say they're religious but no one believes any of that stuff

They do and it makes a big difference to their lives:

'My faith has given me the confidence and motivation to succeed in all aspects of my life. It has encouraged me to treat others with respect and understanding, as they too are part of God's creation.'

Mohammed, Muslim

'My faith has provided me with strength when I've needed it, helped me to tell right from wrong, and given me a way of sorting out what really matters from what doesn't.'

Viren, Jain

Big myth 2: Religious people are just a bunch of fanatics

Turn on the TV and you can see story after story about conflict and problems around the world.

A bomb has gone off. A presenter is saying that religious fanatics are the cause Religion can receive a bad press.

Over the centuries, religious people have stood up for what they believed: from founders of faiths and prophets, to followers like Gandhi and Martin Luther King Jr. Being strong in your views does not make you a 'fanatic'. Believing in the fundamental importance of the teachings of a faith does not make you a 'fundamentalist' in the negative sense of a religious extremist.

Most wars and conflicts have little to do with religion, but religion can get used as a justification by regimes and by terrorists.

'I think religion is being used as a source of conflict and not as a means of worship and everyday guidance as it was when I was younger. This is becoming more of a problem when it never used to be . . . I think somehow we need to find the means whereby Sikhs and Muslims, and Hindus and Muslims, can integrate more and get a better understanding of each other, not seeing a person and just labelling them as a Sikh or Muslim, but seeing the person as they really are.'

Kiran, Sikh

Big myth 3: Religion divides people. All the religions hate each other really

Nothing puts people off like inter religious hatred and squabbling. It's true that there have been centuries of mistrust and out-and-out rivalry. People have sometimes killed or been killed in the name of religion (even though religion may well not have been the actual cause of the problem).

But followers of the different world faith can live together peacefully.

All of the major faiths have teachings which encourage co-operation with people of other faiths.

Across the UK many people of all religions can and do live alongside each other, get on well and work together on practical projects – like helping the homeless or the elderly or improving the local environment. There are many examples of inter-religious harmony even if they rarely make the headlines.

It's time for people of different faiths to speak up louder about all the good things connected with religion: about the ways that religions help people and about the benefits this brings to individuals and communities.

There are over 200 local inter-faith initiatives running in the UK building better inter-faith relations at a local level.*

*source: *Local Inter Faith Activity in the UK: A Survey* published by the Inter Faith Network for the UK 2003.

'*Until different religions take a step back to understand each other, religious conflicts will go on. This is why it is increasingly important for members of different faiths to get on together and to understand the differences between their* beliefs *and practices and, more importantly, to acknowledge the similarities and work side by side to achieve their shared goals.'*

Ashmi, Hindu

■ The above information is from *Connect – different faiths shared values*, a leaflet produced by the Inter Faith Network for the UK in association with TimeBank and the National Youth Agency.

© *The Inter Faith Network*

We need to teach religion

A secular approach to teaching RE risks making a political tool out of faith

Britain is the most irreligious nation in Europe, yet we have compulsory religious education in state schools. No wonder the Government is proposing that the RE curriculum should include non-religious world-views as well as traditional religions.

On an average Sunday, just seven per cent of Britons find their way to church, and a few more to the mosque or temple on other days of the week. At the same time, the Church's traditional role to hatch, match and dispatch our loved ones has been overtaken by designer weddings in trendy venues and funerals with secular celebrants who promise not to mention God.

As a nation, we treat religion like the NHS: we want it there to look after our children and to help us when we are down, but we have virtually no place for it in our personal lives.

Strange, then, that successive governments have refused to abolish the compulsory presence of religion in state schools. RE is still a compulsory part of the national curriculum, although, unlike other subjects, the content is determined by local standing advisory councils for religious education (SACREs).

Recently, the Department for Education published a draft 'national framework' for RE to help the SACREs in drawing up the local curriculum. The draft caused a stir because it says: 'Pupils' own world-

By Christopher Jamison

views, including secular philosophies (for example, Humanism) should be studied, particularly in considering ultimate questions and ethical issues. World views refer to ways of understanding the world that are independent of any religious belief or affiliation.'

On an average Sunday, just seven per cent of Britons find their way to church

If RE involves studying views that are not religious, this immediately raises the question, 'What is RE?' The new framework wants pupils to study the major religions, first Christianity, then Buddhism, Hinduism, Islam, Judaism and Sikhism, as well other religious traditions. So far, so religious. These religions all offer a purpose in life which is divine and is expressed through shared symbols handed down through history.

So what about these 'ways of understanding that are independent of any religious belief'? How can they fit into RE? Well, the answer is, they can't. You cannot claim they are a sort of religion because the whole

point of secular philosophy is to express a purpose in life without reference to the divine. What you see and feel is what you get: that is the essence of secular belief.

Yet secular society is unwilling to let go of RE, and a new irreligious rationale for RE is emerging. We want our children to learn about religion as a way of developing their skills in other areas of life. Through RE, we want them to be spiritually and morally aware, while also wanting them to respect differences. We have no other vehicle that would allow pupils systematically to explore beliefs, right and wrong, life and death. So the aim now is to take over RE and make it serve the needs of the state to generate good, liberal citizens.

The French experience is instructive here. Worried by post-9/11 incomprehension between different groups in French society, Jack Lang, the minister of education, commissioned a report on the teaching of 'religious fact' in secular schools. While staunchly defending the French separation of church and state, he supports more teaching about religion in philosophy and history lessons. This is more honest: he does not want to teach religion in itself, he wants to teach about religion because he fears a lack of social cohesion.

So should clergy like me be grateful that religion is surviving in any form whatsoever in our schools? Not really, because there is another route to offering genuine religious education – that of teaching religion itself. Yet teaching religion is nowadays anathema. After all, goes the secular view, religion is the source of the world's ills: Northern Ireland, the Middle East and Osama bin Laden would all be fine if it wasn't for religion. At the risk of being tortured by the new inquisitors of secular orthodoxy, let me explain why the reverse is true.

To study religion in its own right and on its own terms enables people to consider that there are truths about life that are beyond us, that are sacred and that come from God. We could insist that they study the lives of saints, not as examples of good citizenship but as examples of holiness. If you think that learning about holiness is still vital to our wellbeing, then you will want to prevent the state burying religion under political imperatives such as social cohesion and citizenship.

Of course, our children need philosophical and moral education, but the only way to stop religious fanaticism is to teach religion itself – not to teach about religion

---

The new secular RE is now under the command of our political masters who see in it a useful tool. Yet to see religion in this way runs the risk of using religion for political ends, just as terrorists do. The IRA, Hamas and al-Qa'eda all exploit religion as a convenient cover for their murderous activities. I never met a holy Catholic who set out to blow up a shopping centre and I never met a holy Muslim who crashed aeroplanes into buildings.

Of course, our children need philosophical and moral education, but the only way to stop religious fanaticism is to teach religion itself – not to teach about religion. The best guarantee against perverted religion is true religion, not a course in liberal ethics.

■ The author is Abbot of Worth
© *Telegraph Group Limited, London 2004*

Food rules and religion

Most religions have rules about food. Some religions are stricter than others and within religious groups there will be some followers who are stricter than others. What follows is a rough guide

A rough guide to food rules

In Islam the holy book, the Qur'an, does not permit pork or pork products to be eaten, including pig fat used in the production of other foods. Carnivorous animals are not permitted. Any sea animals which do not have fins or scales (such as crabs, prawns, squid) are considered undesirable by some Muslims. Alcohol in any form is not permitted.

Permissible meat other than pork can only be eaten if it is prepared in the correct way. Prayers must be said during the slaughter and the blood must be able to flow from the animal's body. Meat prepared in the correct way is known as halal meat. During the holy month of Ramadan, Muslims are not allowed to eat from dawn to sunset. However young children, pregnant women and the sick are often exempted.

In Judaism, the Jewish religion, food regulations are known as kashrut. Food which is acceptable is kosher. Kosher food includes animals with split hooves and which chew the cud (including sheep and cows, but not pigs). Most fowl and their eggs are acceptable except birds of prey. Fish is acceptable as long as it has fins and scales. Prawns, crab and squid are not acceptable. Kosher meat must be slaughtered in the correct way by a qualified butcher (known as a shochet). The animal's blood must be allowed to drain from the body through a slit in the throat before being soaked or salted. Jews observe other regulations in food preparation and if you are cooking a meal for Jewish guests it is best to check with them first to make sure what their requirements are.

Hindus are often vegetarians which comes from the principle of ahimsa (not harming). Those who aren't are not permitted to eat beef because the cow is a sacred animal. Strict Hindus will not eat fish or eggs but milk and other dairy products are considered acceptable because no killing has taken place. Many Sikhs are also vegetarian. Those who do eat meat can eat it only if it is jhatka which means the animal has been killed instantly with one stroke. Sikhs are not permitted to eat halal meat or drink alcohol. In Buddhism there are less food restrictions than in some other religions.

However Buddhists will try to avoid intentionally killing. Monks and nuns are usually more strict and some are vegetarians. Others will eat meat if they understand that the animal has not been killed specifically so they can eat. In Chinese forms of Buddhism garlic and onions are avoided because they are thought to heat the blood and make meditation more difficult.

Religion and alcohol

Alcohol is forbidden to Muslims and to followers of a number of other faiths including Baha'i. Many Buddhists, Hindus, Jains and Sikhs and some Christians also choose not to drink alcohol. Some religious people also avoid stimulant drinks that contain caffeine, tea and coffee for example.

■ The above information is from the National Youth Agency's Youth Information website which can be found at www.youthinformation.com
© *National Youth Agency*

The golden rule

A non-religious perspective

All societies and religions have moral principles, laws and rules. Although many of the less important rules vary, all traditions seem to have come up with a version of 'the Golden Rule', 'Do as you would be done by' or 'Treat other people in a way you would like to be treated yourself' – there are more examples below. It can be expressed positively (as above) or negatively ('Do not treat others as you would not like to be treated yourself'). Some people think that the negative versions are better, because it is easier to agree on the things we would not like, and anyone can work out what would cause suffering to themselves or another person and then avoid doing it. For example, you wouldn't want to be bullied, so you shouldn't bully other people.

Humanists are impressed by the fact that we find this very useful basic principle everywhere. It appears to be based on our common humanity, using our need to be treated well by others and our wish to live harmoniously with others as its foundation. It can be worked out by anyone, anywhere, by thinking about our understanding of ourselves and other people. It does not need to be given to us by sacred texts or a god.

The golden rule requires kindness and care for the less fortunate, because this is what we would want in their situation, and it discourages actions like lying and theft because no one wants to be lied to or to have their property stolen. It is simple and clear, and works well in practice.

Examples of the Golden Rule from around the world

'He should treat all beings as he himself should be treated. The essence of right conduct is not to injure anyone.'
(Jainism – from The Suta-Kritanga, about 550 BCE*)

'Do not do to others what you would not like for yourself.'
(Confucianism – from The Analects of Confucius, about 500 BCE)

'I will act towards others exactly as I would act towards myself.'
(Buddhism – from The Siglo-Vada Sutta, about 500 BCE)

'This is the sum of duty: Do nothing to others Which, if done to you, could cause you pain.' (Hinduism – from The Mahabharata, about 150 BCE)

'What you would avoid suffering yourself, seek not to impose on others.'
(Ancient Greece – Epictetus, the Greek philosopher, about 90 CE*)

'Love your neighbour as yourself.'
(Judaism/ Christianity – Leviticus 19, in The Torah, about 400 BCE, quoted by Jesus in Matthew 22 and Mark 12, 1st century CE)

'What is harmful to yourself do not do to your fellow men. That is the whole of the law . . .'
(Judaism – from Hillel: The Talmud, about 100 CE)

'None of you truly believes, until he wishes for his brothers what he wishes for himself.'
(Islam – a saying of the Prophet Muhammad, 7th Century CE)

'As you think of yourself, so think of others.'
(Sikhism – from Guru Granth Sahib, 1604 CE)

One should be 'contented with so much liberty against other men, as he would allow against himself.'
(Great Britain – Thomas Hobbes, English philosopher, 1588-1679 CE)

'He should not wish for others what he does not wish for himself.'
(Baha'i from the writings of Baha'u'llah, about 1870 CE)

'You should always ask yourself what would happen if everyone did what you are doing.'
(France – Jean-Paul Sartre, French existentialist philosopher, 1905-80 CE)

'Treat other people as you'd want to be treated in their situation; don't do things you wouldn't want to have done to you.'
(British Humanist Association, 1999 CE)

* BCE = Before Common Era, equivalent to BC.
CE = Common Era, equivalent to AD.

■ The above information is from the British Humanist Association's website which can be found at www.humanism.org.uk

Wise and wonderful?

Parents and the government alike are fans of faith schools – and of their results. But should schools, as the Archbishop of Canterbury wishes, also be churches? And does their growing popularity mean multicultural education has failed? Wendy Berliner reports

On the classroom door, the notice says that the first person to say welcome is closer to Allah. As the door opens, a class of grinning children in green, white and grey uniforms live up to the spirit of the message with the warmest of welcomes. This is the Al-Aqsa primary school, named after the great mosque in Jerusalem, which educates 85 Leicester children.

Their parents pay up to £1,200 a year to send their children to the school, which is on the site of an Islamic study centre, in two mobile classrooms that have seen better days. Its resources will be nowhere near as good as some of the state schools in Leicester, and the teachers are not formally trained. It's at least 10 miles from the neighbourhood where most Muslims in the area live and the minibuses that bring them here each day cost extra.

But at Al-Aqsa the children get not only the national curriculum but also Arabic, Islamic studies and history, which includes the Muslim influences on the UK, and they can say their prayers in the prayer hall and wear traditional Muslim dress. There are 175 children on the waiting list.

As Ibrahim Hewitt, the school's Geordie headteacher, who converted to Islam more than 20 years ago, says: 'Religion has a role to play in education for families who are believers.' His three children have all come to the school; the youngest is still there.

'Religion has a role to play in education for families who are believers'

On the other side of Leicester, in a muddy field overlooking rolling countryside, workmen are putting in the foundations of the first new Church of England primary school to be built in Leicester for 101 years. It will serve a new estate that will eventually have 1,200 homes, producing a population bigger than a lot of villages. But there will be no church built here. The minister will be based at the school. His office will be across the hall from the head-teacher.

In an outstanding example of the church's new mission to take itself to where the people are, St Mary's will have a sanctuary in the school hall and will be the worship centre for the new community.

In the face of falling con-gregations, schools are increasingly central to the Church of England's mission. The Archbishop of Canter-bury, Dr Rowan Williams, underlined that in his first major address on education last autumn. Encouraging schools to hold their own communion and confirmation services, he said: 'The church school is a church. More is needed in terms of religion in schools than clergy visits and choral services in nearby churches.'

It is the same with Roman Catholic schools. Research at 60 RC secondaries by the Centre for Research and Development in Catholic Education, found that in the face of declining attendance at mass, the RC school is the 'modern living church and parish'.

There will be no fees at St Mary's. It will be funded almost entirely by the public purse, as Anglican and Roman Catholic schools and a minority of the small numbers of other faith schools are. A third of UK schools are faith-based, mainly Anglican and Roman

Catholic, and there are plans for another 100 Church of England secondary schools over the next five years; 62 are already in the pipeline, even though school rolls are falling.

One-quarter of English primary schools have Church of England foundations but there are proportionately few CofE secondaries – the church has 4,500 primaries and just 200 secondary schools. The Roman Catholics have a much more even balance of primary to secondary schools, with 1,760 primary to 363 secondary.

In Leicester, which is likely to become the first city in the UK where the combined ethnic minorities will outnumber the white indigenous population perhaps in less than five years, there is a hardening of the faith lines in education. The faithful have little truck with the melting-pot idea of multiculturalism. They want to see their faiths remain strong in a sea swimming with diverse religious currents. And, encouraged by current government thinking, they are going to get their way.

Jacky Farnell, who will be the first head of St Mary's in Leicester, is currently head of Belgrave St Peter's, another CofE primary in the town, which has just changed its status from controlled to aided to give it more control over admissions and to guarantee its nature as a church school. They have used new legislation to do this, after having to turn away Christian families who wanted places because of restrictions placed on the school by council admissions criteria. The special service to celebrate the change was held at the school last Thursday with the Bishop of Leicester, the Right Rev Tim Stevens, speaking.

Talk to different faith groups in Leicester and you find they are very happy to see each other set up new schools. 'Multiculturalism has largely failed,' says Ibrahim Hewitt. 'We are not all the same. Why should we all be moulded to be the same? It is a very misguided approach. Integration should not be mentioned in a democracy.

'We don't teach hostility to any other faiths. The Koran is a conduit to looking at other faiths. Our kids have to live and work in a society

which they have to know something about. Just celebrating each other's festivals is a very facile approach – it doesn't teach respect. The kids who throw stones at me or spit at me in the street have been through a multicultural education and probably their parents have, but they have no respect for my faith. You could say the educational system has failed them.'

Already there are seven Muslim schools in Leicester, including a secondary school that has just failed to get state funding. The CofE has 94 primaries and three secondaries in the Leicester diocese and is carrying out a feasibility study into a city academy for which it already has a sponsor – a giant food firm that is the largest employer in the county.

'Multiculturalism has largely failed. We are not all the same. Why should we all be moulded to be the same? It is a very misguided approach. Integration should not be mentioned in a democracy.'

The government is keen to see the church get involved in its academy programme because of its reputation for providing successful schools. The church would provide £2m of the cost of the school with the rest – perhaps some £20m – coming from the taxpayer.

But there are many who worry about the rapid growth of faith-based schools and what that might do to social cohesion through the splintering of public and private education along faith, and often racial, lines.

In 2001, the House of Commons education select committee, when looking into school diversity, urged 'extreme caution' on the government over any expansion of the faith-based sector. It pointed to Northern Ireland as an example of how divisions in society could be exacerbated when two communities were further segregated by faith-based schooling. The committee wanted to ensure that any future development of faith-based education should guard against the creation of ethnically segregated schooling.

If this needed any underlining, the Cantle report into riots in Oldham, Bradford and Burnley in 2001 confirmed they were caused at least in part by the split in the ethnic communities in the towns.

The report by Ted Cantle, chairman of the Home Office social cohesion review team, talked about the depth of polarisation caused by segregated communities living parallel lives. Asian children went to schools where most of the children were Asian; white children went to schools where most of the children were white. The two communities were divided and suspicious of each other. Cantle warned that further violence was likely if government, police and community leaders failed to break this polarisation.

One of Cantle's key recommendations, that at least 25% of places at faith-based schools should be available to children of other faiths or none, was not taken up.

Church school populations do differ significantly in their makeup depending on where they are. Roman Catholic schools nationally have 70% of places filled by practising Catholics, but in areas where the school is oversubscribed, particularly in London, this will be 100%. By contrast, some CofE schools in areas where there are substantial ethnic minority populations have rolls that are almost entirely non-Christian.

St Mary's in Leicester will have 51% of its places open to anyone, with the remainder reserved for

Christians or those of other faiths. Canon Peter Taylor, director of education for the Leicester diocese, is at pains to point out how inclusive the new school will be. He does not believe that faith-based schools are a recipe for divided societies.

'My experience is that if you are secure in your own faith position, you are far more likely to understand and respect people of other faith positions,' he says.

Canon John Hall, general secretary of the Church of England board of education, goes further. He believes faith-based schools contribute to community cohesion by helping people of different faiths to feel settled and at home. 'We disagree with those who believe faith schools cause division,' he says.

But the National Secular Society is not convinced. Keith Porteous Wood, general secretary of the society, says: 'Religious schools hamper rather than enhance community and sometimes race relations. It is destructive and undesirable to separate children on religious and sometimes racial grounds, where religious groups also equate to ethnic ones, at this formative time of their lives.

'Children from all religious and racial backgrounds need to get to know each other at school on a day-to-day basis if they are ever to understand and respect each other. Sending them to separate schools can only add to the suspicion, misunderstanding and prejudice that blight the lives of so many.'

Secularists may like to see religion disappear from schools altogether, but the most that is likely to happen is for atheism to be added to the religious studies syllabus, as the Qualifications and Curriculum Authority is suggesting.

Faith-based schools are popular. Often they get the best results in a neighbourhood and have an excellent reputation for discipline, although National Foundation for Educational Research work suggests this has more to do with the favourable quality of their intake than their religious ethos. Church schools can still interview prospective pupils to ensure they and their families will fit in, and around

'Children from all religious and racial backgrounds need to get to know each other at school on a day-to-day basis if they are ever to understand and respect each other'

one in six church schools do this, although the practice will disappear under a new code to be introduced next year. Church of England schools overall have much lower proportions of poor pupils than community schools.

Where faith-based schools are oversubscribed, the children of families who are attending church regularly get first refusal on places, which can boost congregations. London, for example, where there is a dire shortage of places in good state schools, has seen improvements in church attendance, against the national trend.

Anglican schools could be playing a role in the increase in regular Church of England attendance by children and young people (up 1% between 2001 and 2002 after years of decline and against a drop of 100,000 in congregations in the same year). Easter communicants are now a quarter or a third of what they were at the beginning of the 20th century but children and young people up to 16 now make up more than 40% of the Church of England's regular churchgoers.

And church schools are not just popular with parents hunting for good schools. They are popular with the government. David Blunkett, when education secretary, talked about wanting to bottle their magic ingredients. Tony Blair is a fervent fan – he chose faith schools for his own children.

The new suburb of North Hamilton in Leicester, where St Mary's is being constructed, looks typical of the kind of communities being built on greenfield sites throughout the country. There will be social housing, but most of it will be owner-occupied and probably dominated by white families.

Already 17 children are signed up for the embryo school, even though Jacky Farnell doesn't take up her post until Easter and the first children won't be admitted until this autumn. Even then, they will be in mobiles at another primary school. The school building won't be ready to admit its first pupils until next January, but in its purpose-built premises on an attractive new estate, it is bound to be highly popular.

By then the Al-Aqsa school will be in new premises, too. After six years in rented temporary classrooms, it has bought its first permanent building, a redundant Leicester city infants' school. It is much closer to where the majority of the city's Asian community lives. It should go from strength to strength, so that many more Muslim children will be able to greet visitors in unison in Arabic.

How healthy this all is for the unity of the community remains to be seen.

© *Guardian Newspapers Limited 2004*

Humanism becomes one of the new gods of RE

By Liz Lightfoot, Education Correspondent

Humanism, attitudes to sexuality and the ethics of wealth are to be taught alongside Christianity and other faiths in the first national curriculum for religious education.

The national framework published in draft form 27 April 2004 was welcomed by the Church of England but the Catholic Education Service said there was more work to be done to ensure it did not turn into 'a sociology of religions'.

Representatives from all of Britain's main religions had advised the Qualifications and Curriculum Authority as it made its first attempt to provide a common framework for RE lessons.

But some Christian groups said the document 'betrayed' Christianity by its emphasis on comparing different religions and examining 'secular faiths' such as humanism.

Religious education must be taught in all state schools but parents have the right to withdraw their children. Governors of church schools will remain in charge of their RE lessons, and the new framework is voluntary for all schools.

The draft says Christianity must be taught throughout a child's time at school but in order to provide balanced education there must be study of the other principal religions in Britain, other world religious traditions and pupils' own world views 'including secular philosophies, for example humanism'.

Pupils should not just learn about religion but learn from religion by being taught to 'reflect and evaluate their own and others' beliefs about world issues such as peace and conflict, wealth and poverty and the importance of the environment'.

RE teachers are also urged to 'promote other aspects of the curriculum' such as financial capability through considering the ethics of wealth, debt, poverty, gambling and business.

They should also promote personal, social and health education by looking at religious beliefs on such issues as 'relationships and human sexuality' and sex education.

Fred Naylor, spokesman for the Parental Alliance for Choice in Education, said Christianity was being 'betrayed'.

'Christianity is a fundamental part of our history and tradition and

> 'Of course pupils should be told about other faiths, but in a factual way and not as part of a sociological study of religions'

yet it is being portrayed as no more important to schoolchildren in Britain than other world religions. The result is a multi-cultural mish-mash.'

The Campaign for Real Education said most parents wanted their children taught about their own faith. 'Of course pupils should be told about other faiths, but in a factual way and not as part of a sociological study of religions.'

The Church of England Board of Education said children were to be taught about Christianity from the age of three to 19. 'There is a very strong commitment to the teaching of Christianity,' said Canon John Hall, its chief education officer.

'It does not talk about atheism but it talks about humanism. You can't talk about faiths without also recognising ... there will be children in the class or their parents who do not believe in God.'

What we believe in now

Which, if any, of the following would you say best describes you?

Description	Percentage
I am a practising member of an organised religion	18%
I am a non-practising member of an organised religion	25%
I am spiritually inclined but don't really 'belong' to an organised religion	24%
I am agnostic (not sure if there's a God)	14%
I am atheist (convinced there's no God)	12%
None of these	7%
Don't know	1%

Source: Three In Five 'Believe in God', 8-17 August 2003. MORI

Should faith-based projects try to promote their beliefs?

The Catholic youth service is developing a covenant for its work with young people that will define the role evangelisation should play within its youth work projects across England and Wales.

Yes – Phil Hulks, director of national ministries, Crusaders

Young people have the right to know about faith so they can make an informed choice. There is a difference between giving people the hard sell and providing information on something you believe is right to help others make up their own minds.

Going out into the community is a great opportunity for young people to demonstrate their beliefs, because actions speak louder than words.

We would encourage that and if the opportunity arises to discuss it then that is OK. If you are not allowed to discuss your faith with others, then it can lead to an integrity gap. If as Christians we hide and don't give people a chance to find out about our faith, we are not doing anyone any favours. Evangelism is important to Crusaders, but there's a way to do it and a way not to do it.

Yes – Farid Ali, president, Swansea Muslim Youth League

At a time when the world seems more hostile than ever before, active participation in the community is critical. If we are proud to say that today Britain is a multicultural society, then this multiculturalism must be preserved and encouraged.

The 2001 census revealed that most migrated communities are faith-based.

Faith-based groups and projects connect the vast majority of Black and minority ethnic communities to their roots. They have done a great job in developing greater understanding with the wider community.

We can no longer view the world as we did before 11 September 2001. Things have changed, and everyone needs to redouble their efforts in building that bridge that has been so damaged. If there are no faith-based groups from all sides, how then are we to develop the tolerant and understanding society that everyone craves? How are we to preserve the multicultural Britain that we are so proud of? It is crucial that faith-based projects and groups promote their culture and faith to develop awareness and greater understanding.

No – Marilyn Mason, education officer, British Humanist Association

It depends on whether the youth project is publicly or privately funded.

If it is publicly funded then it should be inclusive and not promote a religion. If it is self-financed then it's OK.

We have an ongoing issue with the Scouts and Girlguiding UK in that they take public funding but they exclude atheists. Scouts and Guides have to swear to serve their God, whichever one that is, but young atheists are not allowed to be part of it. We write to them two or three times a year about it but they say they are within their rights. When it comes to funding, it is not the State's job to promote religion or a culture that tries to convert others or discriminates against other religions, so all publicly funded youth groups to do with faith can be considered discriminatory.

Yes – Reverend Les Isaac, Ascension Trust Street Pastor Initiative

Yes, but the context is crucial when it comes to promoting religion.

When street pastors go out to help young people, some might ask us why we are doing what we are doing. In this case, I would take the opportunity to talk about my faith and explain that it teaches and challenges me to love my neighbour and want to help them.

Some people aren't ready to hear it but others are. In the context of church youth work, it should be about teaching the principles of the religion, how and what people believe, and the practicalities of living the religion.

Faith projects for young people are not well funded for some reason, as opposed to education or health. But the reality is that spirituality is a big part of a person and people want morals and values.

After the shootings in Birmingham, the churches were full of young people.

Their spirits were crying out for something to help them. You can't underestimate their intelligence. The promotion of religion should be in context. We say it is not about preaching but about caring, listening and helping young people and praying for them.

■ The above information is from *Young People Now* magazine, 29 September 2004. For more information visit their website: www.ypnmagazine.com

> **Britain is a multicultural society, then this multiculturalism must be preserved and encouraged**

Lure of the celebrity sect

During an exclusive tour of Scientology's Celebrity Centre, Jamie Doward quizzed personnel about the church's teachings

For a second or so the needle proceeds smoothly along the dial. I watch its progress while clutching two can-shaped metal devices, wired to the small machine housing the dial. Suddenly, the needle jerks violently.

'What was that?' asks Janet Laveau, head of the UK Office of Special Affairs, the Church of Scientology's PR machine. I'm disturbed and temporarily impressed – the needle jumped just as I was thinking of a friend who is seriously depressed. How could the machine 'know' what I was thinking?

Few people outside the Church of Scientology, which this year celebrates its 50th anniversary, have seen the E-meter. And fewer still have road-tested it at the Scientology Celebrity Centre in Bayswater, London, a stucco-fronted building where the church's many celebrity followers study the religion when in the capital.

The device is said to measure the mental state of a person, allowing the church's teachers – known as auditors – to pinpoint areas of concern. It would not seem out of place on *Star Trek*. And, to many, the idea of a church erecting specialist centres for celebrities must seem deeply alien.

But then, the church, which for decades has been at the centre of lawsuits and government investigations, is no stranger to controversy.

Now, however, the church has allowed *The Observer* access to its Celebrity Centre, although it didn't allow photographs. For the first time, a British newspaper could quiz its senior personnel about its finances, beliefs and influence on wider society.

The picture that emerges is of a sophisticated, well-organised church that is a bizarre marriage of Hollywood and hi-tech.

This is largely down to its founder. The religion – and

numerous experts agree that it is a religion – was founded by Lafayette Ronald Hubbard, a globe-trotting autodidact who funded his research into what became Scientology by writing a series of best-selling novels.

Hubbard, who died in 1986, credits psychoanalysts such as Freud with influencing his early work, but the 40 million or so words he produced which shape Scientology's teachings today draw on a panoply of interests, ranging from nuclear physics to engineering to anthropology.

Hubbard's influence is everywhere in the Celebrity Centre. His words are written in bold lettering on the walls. Numerous photographs show him as a chubby man with a receding hairline in a tank top and slacks, gazing enigmatically into the distance.

And then there is Hubbard's vacant office. Every Scientology Celebrity Centre across the world has a sealed room devoted to Hubbard, kept vacant as a mark of respect. In London, a sturdy walnut desk, on which stands Hubbard's name-plate, takes centre stage.

But what you won't see on the office walls, or any other Scientology building for that matter, is Hubbard's FBI file. You won't see the letters Hubbard wrote to the US secret services offering his help in the battle against communism. You won't read the letters he wrote denouncing associates as communists, and you won't see the file in which one agent referred to him as a 'mental case'.

And you also won't read any of the negative publicity the religion has attracted, such as the repeated charge that Scientology narrows people's consciousness. Scientologists fiercely rebut such charges, arguing that the church's teachings give its followers a true sense of freedom, empowering them to take control of their lives.

But the government, aware of concerns surrounding Scientology, refuses to recognise the church's claim for charitable status, as happens in a number of countries, including the US.

And yet, despite the negative publicity it has drawn over the past half-century, Scientology has a powerful draw for many people. The church says it has nine million followers in 156 countries. It has 3,700 churches, missions and groups, administered by more than 16,000 staff worldwide. It claims it has 118,000 Scientologists in the UK alone.

Critics dispute the claims. But what is irrefutable is that Scientology has powerful friends who give it global influence. Each year it holds a celebrity gala for the likes of Tom Cruise and John Travolta, which is attended by thousands and makes for great PR. Other celebrity followers include the actress Juliette Lewis and Nancy Cartwright, the voice of Bart Simpson.

Scientologists believe that celebrities wield enormous influence because they are copied by their fans. 'A culture is only as great as its dreams and its dreams are dreamed by artists,' runs one Scientology maxim.

In the US, senior politicians, civic leaders and police officers line up to sing its praises. The church's work on drug rehabilitation and curbing recidivism has earned it plaudits from those in the penal system. 'I know of no other group doing more effective work in combating the problem of drug abuse,' says Chris Brightmore, a retired detective chief superintendent at Scotland Yard, in one Scientology pamphlet.

The actress Kirstie Alley says Scientology's drug rehab programme, called Narconon, 'salvaged my life and began my acting career'. And in terms of formulating social policy, Scientology has had some stunning successes.

A campaign, spearheaded by another celebrity Scientologist, Lisa Marie Presley, resulted in a major backlash against schools injecting children who had attention deficit disorder with the drug Ritalin. The church's applied scholastics programme has produced scores of converts in Africa and the developing world. At least one private school in the UK is also said to use the system.

It appears an impressive track record for a religion started only half a century ago. Its success is down to the fact that Scientology claims to hold answers to everyday problems. Scientologists believe that people strive to be good and try to help them achieve this. Followers like to quote Hubbard's maxim: 'Others talk about a better world. We are making one.'

There is a strong neo-liberal vein, placing responsibility firmly on individuals to help themselves and then help others.

One of Scientology's aims is for followers to achieve a state of 'Clear', when a person loses all fears, anxieties and irrational thoughts. Beyond this, followers can progress to a series of levels about which little is known, simply because few people ever train long enough to reach them.

However a number of ex-followers have talked about the training they received to detach what Scientologists call 'Body Thetans'. These, according to Hubbard, relate back to the 'Xenu incident' which occurred 75 million years ago. Back then Xenu, who was apparently the Galactic Federation ruler, dropped thousands of human souls into volcanoes on Hawaii and in the Mediterranean and then blew them up with hydrogen bombs. The disembodied souls – known as Body Thetans – exist today and produce warped thoughts among humans. Only by following Hubbard's writings, say Scientologists, can they be removed.

One of Scientology's aims is for followers to achieve a state of 'Clear', when a person loses all fears, anxieties and irrational thoughts

---

For obvious reasons, the church does not like to talk about the 'Xenu incident'. Supporters say it assumes true meaning only after years of study and complain that those opposed to Scientology use it to paint a derogatory picture of the religion as little more than a sci-fi fantasy, akin to Hubbard's novels.

That numerous organisations have taken a dim view of Scientology is no surprise to its followers. They argue that there are scores of vested interests which feel threatened by Scientology's success.

Over the years, the church has used the freedom of information act to produce a vast library of what it says is incontrovertible evidence that

official agencies have conspired against it.

'I'm well aware of the controversy and where it comes from,' said Laveau. 'It all started in the 1950s, when Mr Hubbard started Dianetics [the precursor to Scientology]. Our programmes get people off drugs, they stop ex-prisoners committing new crimes. Other organisations get billions in funding and, if they get a 2 per cent result, that's a success. We get between 70 and 80 per cent success rates. Any group that's effective is going to stir up controversy.'

It is also going to make a lot of money. Unlike other religions, followers of Scientology pay for their training, as do schools that want to use its Applied Scholastics programme and those who want Narconon counselling. The fact that many countries have given the religion charitable status helps, but supporters are quick to dismiss claims that Scientology is a giant money-making business. 'An initial course costs just £16. And all the life improvement courses cost under £50,' Laveau said.

Further up the chain, though, the courses become more expensive, something that the church justifies on its website. 'When one considers the cost of delivering even one hour of auditing, requiring extensively trained specialists, and the overhead costs of maintaining church premises, the necessity of donations becomes clear.'

For those who seek enlightenment, Scientology certainly doesn't come cheap. It is estimated that a dedicated follower can spend tens of thousands.

But those who claim Scientology's training has given them greater confidence, inner strength and, ultimately, happiness, are more than willing to pay the price.

As a best-selling pulp fiction writer once noted: 'If a man really wants to make a million dollars, the best way would be to start his own religion.' The writer? L. Ron Hubbard.

■ This article first appeared in *The Observer*, 16 May 2004.

© *Guardian Newspapers Limited 2004*

New religious movements

Information from INFORM

What are NRMs?

New Religious Movements (NRMs), alternative religions, sects or cults all have technical definitions in the literature of the social sciences. Here, however, the subject is widely defined as groups which (a) have become visible in their present form since the Second World War, and (b) are religious in so far as they offer an answer to some of the ultimate questions traditionally addressed by mainstream religions: Is there a God? What is the purpose of life? What happens to us after death? This definition includes atheistic 'religions' and philosophies such as various forms of Buddhism, and part of the Human Potential movement, which enjoins its members to search for 'the god within'. While scholars tend to use neutral terms, such as NRM, minority or alternative religion, the media and general public usually employ the word 'cult', which has negative overtones, often implying bizarre beliefs, sinister and deceptive practices, mind control or psychological coercion and, perhaps, sexual abuse and violent tendencies. Among the better-known such movements frequently referred to as 'cults' in this more popular sense are the Unification Church (the 'Moonies'), the International Society for Krishna Consciousness (the Hare Krishna), Scientology, the Rajneesh movement and The Family (once known as the Children of God).

Diversity among NRMs

New religions have, of course, appeared throughout history – early Christianity was a new religion, so were Islam and Methodism at their conception. Nineteenth-century NRMs such as the Jehovah's Witnesses and Mormons nearly all shared something with the Judaeo-Christian tradition; the present wave, however, includes not only movements containing aspects of Christianity, Islam, Hinduism, Buddhism or Shinto, but various combinations of these, plus a motley assortment of ideas from such sources as psychoanalysis, science fiction, NeoPaganism and Satanism. As well as the variety of beliefs, there is also an enormous diversity in their practices, organisation, life-styles and the effects NRMs can have on both individuals and society. Leaders may be seen as gurus, prophets, messiahs, gods or goddesses. Members may be old or young, black or white, rich or poor. Some live in remote rural communes, some in suburban semi-detacheds, and others in inner-city apartments. They may indulge in sexual orgies or lead ascetic lives of strict celibacy. Practices range from chanting, prayer, meditation or dance to ritual sacrifice. The size of the movement may be hundreds of thousands or no more than a handful – and, just as in the Catholic Church one finds priests, devoted believers, occasional worshippers and nominal members, NRMs may have several levels of membership ranging from the most committed to casual sympathisers. Some movements are actually or potentially harmful; others are perfectly benign. In short, almost the only generalisation that one can make is that they have been labelled an NRM or a cult at one time or other.

> *New religions have, of course, appeared throughout history – early Christianity was a new religion, so were Islam and Methodism at their conception*

Changes in NRMs

It is obvious enough, although frequently forgotten, that new religions are likely to change far more rapidly than older religions. Converts become older and more mature. Second and subsequent generations demand the resources of both time

Characteristics associated with NRMs

There are, nonetheless, some characteristics that tend to be found in any movement that is both new and religious. First, almost by definition, the members are first-generation converts, and, like all converts, they tend to be far more enthusiastic and committed – even fanatical – than those born into their religion. Secondly, the membership tends to be atypical of society as a whole, with the movements that became visible around the 1970s appealing disproportionately (though not exclusively) to young, well-educated, middle-class whites, unencumbered by responsibilities such as children or mortgage payments. Thirdly, the founder or leader often wields charismatic authority – that is, he (or sometimes she) is accorded by followers the right to pronounce on all aspects of their life: whom they marry, whether they have children, what sort of work they should do, what sort of clothes they should wear and food they may eat, where they should live, perhaps even whether they should live. Being unbounded by tradition or rules, charismatic leaders tend to be unpredictable and unaccountable to anyone except, perhaps, God. Fourthly, new religions tend to have far more clear-cut versions of The Truth than older religions, which have accommodated to the interests of successive generations. Fifthly, there is frequently a sharp distinction made by NRMs between 'us' and 'them', the former being seen as homogeneously good and godly, the latter as homogeneously bad and, perhaps, satanic. Sixthly, there is often suspicion and/or antagonism from the wider society to which the group offers an alternative.

and money, and frequently question the movements' beliefs and practices. Founders die and the authority structure is likely to become more bureaucratic and predictable. Beliefs, especially empirical beliefs and prophecies such as the arrival of the millennium, may have to be adapted, reinterpreted or changed, and divisions between members and non-members will tend to become less starkly demarcated. Related to such changes and the fact that the movement may become more familiar and thus less frightening to non-members, some of the antagonisms may diminish – although this is by no means always the case.

Joining an NRM

Why, it has often been asked, would well-educated people with promising careers in front of them give it all up, cut off from ties of family and friends to work long hours making money for an exploitative leader while they themselves live in poverty, with little or no control over their own lives? One popular answer that usefully absolves both converts and their families from any responsibility is that they were 'brainwashed' or subjected to irresistible and irreversible manipulative techniques.

It is perfectly true that several of the movements, like most evangelical groups who believe that they must convince others of their Truth, do put considerable pressure on potential members – they may 'love-bomb' (overwhelm with praise and affection), isolate and/or induce guilt or employ various other methods, including deception about their true identity. It is also true, however, that these methods (a) do not differ from those used in many other situations in society, and (b) are not nearly as successful as either the movements themselves would wish or their opponents would have us believe.

In the late 1970s, when accusations about the brainwashing prowess of 'Moonies' were at their height, I studied over a thousand people who had become interested enough in the Unification Church to attend one of their residential weekend workshops where the supposedly irresistible mind control

occurred. I found that over 90% of the workshop attendees, despite the pressure, decided that they did not wish to join. Furthermore, the majority of those who did join left, of their own free will, within a couple of years. Since then many other scholars have found a similar outcome when other groups have been attempting to recruit new members, although such findings tend to be denied by the NRMs (which do not wish anyone to realise how unsatisfied the converts can become), and by the movements' opponents (who wish to further the brainwashing thesis to illustrate the control the movements have over their 'victims').

If the brainwashing/mind-control explanation is not satisfactory in the light of the evidence, what explanations might we offer instead? Social scientists who have studied conversions to NRMs

have observed a far more subtle interplay between the individual and the group, and insist that, given the wide range of different movements and different individuals who join them, no single explanation can suffice. While the vast majority of people are unlikely to join any alternative religion, some might join a particular kind of NRM, and others might be attracted to a quite different kind. A few might be persuaded to join almost any group – but such people tend to leave and possibly join another group within a relatively short period of time.

The important point to be drawn from the fact that members of NRMs are incapable of recruiting and/or keeping all those upon whom they bestow their time and energy (including some of their own children) is that what they offer only 'works' for some people. In other words, if we want to understand what is going on, we have to look not only at the purported attractions of the movement, but also at the individuals who join. It may be that the person is escaping from something – perhaps from a loving but over-possessive family, an unhappy partnership or an uninteresting or unpromising career. They may believe that the traditional religions are dull, boring, hypocritical and apathetic, and/or that life in the wider society has little to offer them apart from the opportunity to be a cog in a vast, impersonal and materialistic rat race.

The challenge of NRMs?

How might those with responsibilities for young adults prepare them for encounters with NRMs? Neither ignorance nor over-sensationalised 'atrocity tales' are helpful. The most effective preparation is education – to ensure not only that people are aware of potential problems associated with some NRMs, but also that they are aware of the attractions that the movements might have to offer. The attraction might be no more than the opportunity in a secular world to talk about theological and/or moral questions; it might be the offer of a chance to make the world a better place, or to develop better relationships. Teachers and youth leaders can organise group discussions in which questions raised by NRMs are seriously considered. Most people would like the world to be better, but is giving up one's career to serve a guru necessarily the best way to achieve this goal? Are there alternative means of developing one's potential or creating better relationships with one's fellow beings than those proposed by the group? There might also be discussions (which can include role-playing) that could lead to a heightened awareness of the sorts of ways in which one might become unduly influenced – not so much by strange mind-control techniques as by, say, the enthusiastic idealism of a movement's members.

Others may be 'seekers', looking for (or susceptible to the suggestion that they are looking for) a closer relationship with God, or a better world (perhaps they are persuaded that they can play a role in bringing the Kingdom of Heaven on earth). Perhaps they are attracted to the idea of belonging to a friendly community of like-minded people, sharing values that they believe to be absent in the wider society. Others find attraction in the promise that they can develop their careers or their relationships through discovering their 'true selves'.

Dangers associated with NRMs

While the movements offer a variety of attractions, they do not always deliver what they have promised, and there may well be downsides to membership of a new religion. Before discussing these, a word of caution might be helpful. Since the early 1970s, there has been the growth of an 'anti-cult' movement (ACM) which is devoted to controlling, banning or at least warning people about the dangers of NRMs. Anti-cultists differ significantly from each other, some are relatives who have suffered extreme anxiety and frustration at 'losing' a loved one to a movement; sometimes they are professionals who have a financial interest in defining NRMs as unambiguously bad and dangerous. Because of its antagonistic approach towards the movements, the ACM tends to ignore or dismiss their more normal or positive aspects, and select only the most negative stories about NRMs, frequently feeding these to the media, which have an interest in disseminating sensational stories, which most of us find more fascinating than stories about everyday, normal phenomena. Because unacceptable actions by members of 'bizarre cults' are much more likely to be reported than the same actions by non-members, we frequently assume that criminal or anti-social acts we learn about are typical of NRMs and atypical of the rest of society. While one may see a headline 'Cult member kills himself', one is very unlikely to see one announcing 'Anglican kills himself', despite the fact that the rate of suicides among the general population could be twice that of the NRM in question.

There are undoubtedly instances when members have been murdered or committed suicide (the media constantly remind us of the tragic examples of Jonestown, the Solar Temple, Aum Shinrikyo and Heaven's Gate). But it should be noted that the vast majority of the thousand or so NRMs in Britain do not indulge in such horrible behaviour, and that many deaths have been brought about in the name of old religions.

While the movements offer a variety of attractions, they do not always deliver what they have promised

---

None the less, when NRMs exhibit characteristics such as insisting that they, the chosen ones, alone have the truth; when leaders lack any accountability and there are authority structures requiring unquestioning obedience and encouraging a growing dependency upon the movements for material, spiritual and social resources, and/or (especially) when groups cut themselves off from the rest of society (geographically and/or socially), these should be recognised as signs of potential danger. Actual problems may vary from movement to movement – one may demand its members' money, another exploit their labour power; one may expect its members to lead a life of celibacy, another that they indulge in sexual orgies. Some NRMs induce fear and feelings of guilt; others remove all sense of responsibility. And, occasionally, an NRM might persuade its members to commit acts of deception, cruelty and/or crime.

What if a student, relative or friend does join an NRM?

Perhaps the most important thing that relatives, friends and those concerned about someone who has joined an NRM should do is to keep in touch with the convert, thereby enabling him or her to have access to

New religious movements – members in the UK	
Christian Groups	
The Church of Jesus Christ of Latter-day Saints	178,059 (as of 2003)
Jehovah's Witnesses	120,000 (as of 2004)
Jesus Fellowship Church aka Jesus Army	2,681 (as of 2000)
Family Federation for World Peace and Unification	550
The Family (formerly known as The Children of God)	8,048 full time (as of 2002)
The Universal Church of the Kingdom of God	4,500 (as of 2001)
The Exclusive Brethren	15,000 (as of 2003)
The Iona Community	232 full time members (as of 2001)
Redeemed Christian Church of God, an African Independent Church	200,000 (as of 2000)
Gilbert Deya Ministries, an African Independent Church	36,000 (as of 2004)
Islamic Groups	
Hizb-ut-Tahrir	refuses to disclose
Al-Muhajiroun	6,500-7,000 (as of 2001)
Buddhist Groups	
Soka Gakkai International (SGI)	5,000 approx
New Kadampa Tradition (NKT)	3,000-6,000 in Europe approx
Friends of the Western Buddhist Order (FWBO)	670 (order members)
Hindu Groups	
Brahma Kumaris World Spiritual University	1,500 (as of 2004)
Sai Baba	4,000 (as of 1999)
School of Economic Science (SES)	2,500 (as of 2004 approx)
Transcendental Meditation (TM)	No members as such but 200,000 people have learnt TM
Sahaja Yoga	750 (as of 2000)
International Society for Krishna Consciousness (ISKCON)	13,000 (associate members)
Osho Movement	1,000 (in 2004)
Other groups	
The Pagan Federation	5,000 (international membership in 2000)
The Aetherius Society	700 full members
Adidam	80 active members (as of 2004)
Falun Gong	170 members (as of 2004)
Sukyo Mahikari	300 (as of 2004)
The Template Foundation	about 300 (as of 2004)
Subud	1,360 (as of 2000)
Theosophical Society	1,020 (as of 2000)
	Source: Various. Inform

alternative versions of reality. While one does not have to agree with the convert's decision, it is not helpful either to cut off all communication or to bombard him or her with accusations and/or dire warnings about the 'evils of destructive cults'. Lack of information and misinformation can both result in inappropriate actions and it is sensible to get as much knowledge and understanding as possible about both the particular movement and the individual concerned – his or her fears, aspirations, current situation etc. –

and thus, perhaps, be able to suggest an alternative to life in the movement. Occasionally it might be advisable to elicit the help of the social services or the law. It is, however, also necessary to recognise that in a democratic, pluralist society adults have the right to make their own choices about what they believe and how they should live their lives – so long, of course, that they do not offend against the laws of the land.

■ Eileen Barker, FBA, OBE, Professor Emeritus of Sociology with Special Reference to the Study of Religion at the London School of Economics, is the founder and Chair of Inform, a charity supported by the Home Office and mainstream Churches that provides information about minority religions. Her 220 publications include the award-winning *The Making of a Moonie: Brainwashing or Choice?* and *New Religious Movements: A Practical Introduction*. For further information, visit Inform's website: www.lse.ac.uk/collections/INFORM

© Inform

What is a cult?

Information from the Cult Information Centre

Every cult can be defined as a group having all of the following five characteristics:

1. It uses psychological coercion to recruit, indoctrinate and retain its members.
2. It forms an elitist totalitarian society.
3. Its founder leader is self-appointed, dogmatic, messianic, not accountable and has charisma.
4. It believes 'the end justifies the means' in order to solicit funds and recruit people.
5. Its wealth does not benefit its members or society.

Are cults harmful?
To remain within the strict mental and social confines of a cult for even a short time can have the following disastrous effects:

- Loss of choice and free will.
- Diminished intellectual ability, vocabulary and sense of humour.
- Reduced use of irony, abstractions and metaphors.
- Reduced capacity to form flexible and intimate relationships.
- Poor judgement.
- Physical deterioration.
- Malnutrition.
- Hallucinations, panic, dissociation, guilt, identity diffusion and paranoia.
- Neurotic, psychotic or suicidal tendencies.

Categories of cults

Religious cults	Therapy cults
Communal living common.	Communal living rare.
Members may leave or not join society's workforce.	Members usually stay in society's workforce.
Average age at the point of recruitment is in the 20s.	Average age at the point of recruitment is in the mid 30s
Registered as religious groups.	Registered as 'non profit making' groups.
Appear to offer association with a group interested in making the world a better place via political, spiritual or other means.	Appear to offer association with a group giving courses in some kind of self-improvement or self-help technique or therapy.

Caring, loving, wholesome individuals and groups do exist. The call, however, is for discernment and a need to fully question all interesting groups before becoming involved and/or a member.

What is mind control?
Mind control techniques include:

Hypnosis
Inducing a state of high suggestibility by hypnosis, often thinly disguised as relaxation or meditation.

Peer group pressure
Suppressing doubt and resistance to new ideas by exploiting the need to belong.

Love bombing
Creating a sense of family and belonging through hugging, kissing, touching and flattery.

Rejection of old values
Accelerating acceptance of new life style by constantly denouncing former values and beliefs.

Confusing doctrine
Encouraging blind acceptance and rejection of logic through complex lectures on an incomprehensible doctrine.

Metacommunication
Implanting subliminal messages by stressing certain key words or phrases in long, confusing lectures.

Removal of privacy
Achieving loss of ability to evaluate logically by preventing private contemplation.

Time sense deprivation
Destroying ability to evaluate information, personal reactions, and

body functions in relation to passage of time by removing all clocks and watches.

Disinhibition
Encouraging child-like obedience by orchestrating child-like behaviour.

Uncompromising rules
Inducing regression and disorientation by soliciting agreement to seemingly simple rules which regulate mealtimes, bathroom breaks and use of medications.

Verbal abuse
Desensitising through bombardment with foul and abusive language.

Sleep deprivation and fatigue
Creating disorientation and vulnerability by prolonging mental and physical activity and withholding adequate rest and sleep.

Dress codes
Removing individuality by demanding conformity to the group dress code.

Chanting and singing
Eliminating non-cult ideas through group repetition of mind-narrowing chants or phrases.

Confession
Encouraging the destruction of individual ego through confession of personal weaknesses and innermost feelings of doubt.

Financial commitment
Achieving increased dependence on the group by 'burning bridges' to the past, through the donation of assets.

Finger pointing
Creating a false sense of righteousness by pointing to the shortcomings of the outside world and other cults.

Flaunting hierarch
Promoting acceptance of cult authority by promising advancement, power and salvation.

Isolation
Inducing loss of reality by physical separation from family, friends, society and rational references.

Controlled approval
Maintaining vulnerability and confusion by alternately rewarding and punishing similar actions.

Change of diet
Creating disorientation and

increased susceptibility to emotional arousal by depriving the nervous system of necessary nutrients through the use of special diets and/or fasting.

Games
Inducing dependence on the group by introducing games with obscure rules.

No questions
Accomplishing automatic acceptance of beliefs by discouraging questions.

Guilt
Reinforcing the need for 'salvation' by exaggerating the sins of the former lifestyles.

Fear
Maintaining loyalty and obedience to the group by threatening soul, life or limb for the slightest 'negative' thought, word or deed.

Replacement of relationships
Destroying pre-cult families by arranging cult marriages and 'families'.

> 'When you meet the friendliest people you have ever known, who introduce you to the most loving group of people you've ever encountered, and you find the leader to be the most inspired, caring, compassionate and understanding person you've ever met, and then you learn the cause of the group is something you never dared hope could be accomplished, and all of this sounds too good to be true – it probably is too good to be true! Don't give up your education, your hopes and ambitions to follow a rainbow.'
>
> Jeannie Mills. Ex-member of The People's Temple, later found murdered.

Who do cults recruit?
Cults want people who are:
- Intelligent.
- Idealistic.
- Well educated.
- Economically advantaged.
- Intellectually or spiritually curious.
- Any age.

How do I avoid the cults?
Cults use sophisticated mind control techniques that will work on anyone, given the right circumstances. Those who think they are immune are only making themselves more vulnerable. Remember the assault is on your emotions, not on your intellect.

The two basic principles of psychological coercion are:
1. If you can make a person *behave* the way you want, you can make that person *believe* the way you want.
2. Sudden, drastic changes in environment lead to heightened suggestibility and to drastic changes in attitudes and beliefs.

Beware!
Protect yourself! Why go away for a weekend or longer with a stranger or a strange group unless:
- You know the name of the sponsoring group.
- You know its ideas, beliefs and affiliations.
- You know what is going to happen at the gathering.
- You know what will be expected of you.
- You know that you will be free and able to leave at any time.

How do I help a cult member? – the dos and don'ts

The dos

- Do try to keep in regular contact via mail or telephone even if there is little response.
- Do express sincere love for the cult member at every available opportunity.
- Do keep a diary of comments, attitudes and events associated with his/her life in the cult.
- Do always welcome the cult member back into the family home no matter what is said.
- Do keep copies of all written correspondence from you and the individual.
- Do record all the names, addresses and phone numbers of people linked with the cult.
- Do try to bite your tongue if the cult member makes unkind comments.
- Do read all of the recommended books relating to cults and mind control, as well as reading other information on the cult in question.
- Do seek help and information from organisations specialising in counter-cult work. We care about you and your individual situation.

The don'ts

- Do not rush into adopting a potential solution before carefully researching the cult problem.
- Do not say: 'You are in a cult; you are brainwashed.'
- Do not give money to the member of the group.
- Do not feel guilty. This is not a problem caused by families.
- Do not act in an angry or hostile manner towards the cult member.
- Do not feel alone. It happens to thousands of families every year.
- Do not underestimate the control the cult has over a member.
- Do not antagonise the cult member by ridiculing his/her beliefs.
- Do not be judgemental or confrontational towards the cult member.
- Do not antagonise any of the cult's leadership or members.
- Do not be persuaded by a cult 'specialist' to pay large sums of money without verifying his/her qualifications.
- Do not give up hope of success in helping your family member to leave the group no matter how long the involvement has already been
- Do not neglect yourself or other family members.

■ The above information is from the Cult Information Centre's website: www.cultinformation.co.uk

© by kind permission of the Cult Information Centre

Let us prey

Many new students starting university are curious and idealistic. Which makes them vulnerable to the increasing number of cults targeting campuses, reports Lynne Wallis

Few parents will consider it necessary to warn their children about the dangers of mind control cults as they leave for university, but perhaps they should. Cults and new religious movements are looking increasingly to university students as a potential pool of devotees, and autumn is the prime time for recruitment. Ian Haworth of the Cult Information Centre says that the numbers of cults recruiting from universities has almost certainly increased – they estimate that there are 500 cult movements active in the UK today. 'They look for intelligent, idealistic, young people, and students meet their criteria in every way. Add to that the fact that they will be disorientated, in a totally new environment with nothing familiar around them, and they are a perfect target for these groups.

'Universities need to be more aware of the dangers, because the

groups will rarely identify themselves as what they really are until it's too late, and they can seem so plausible.'

Involvement with a cult can cause lasting damage. Sarah Cope-Faulkner, now 34, became a member of the now disbanded International

Church of Christ during her second year at Edinburgh University in the early 90s. A member of the Christian union, she lost friends after her first year when various fallings-out occurred and she found herself in a shared house with strangers. When 'Jodie' invited her to a Bible study group, she found herself flattered by the offer of friendship from this slim, pretty young woman in jeans and trainers, and was touched by her apparent care and interest.

'The atmosphere at the events I went to was angelic,' says Cope-Faulkner, 'and I thought, "Wow, all these people want to know little old me." It was all "Amen" and "Come on, sister" and I wanted more. The only way to have more was to continue Bible study. That's when they get you to make a sin list, and what they put me through was so black and bad I wanted to kill myself. They were still being lovely, saving me, and they said I had to redeem myself and repent which meant becoming a full member.'

Baptised in a cold garage in a freezing paddling pool, Sarah thought she had cracked it and found the key to everlasting life. Instead, it was the beginning of a miserable two years that ended in her abandoning her studies, getting into serious debt through all the donations she had to make to the cult, and having a full nervous breakdown.

She remembers: 'I attended 20 meetings a week and became estranged from my family and friends. I was up at 4am for Bible study, and I spent all my time trying to please everyone. If I recruited someone and Jodie liked me again, I would feel utterly elated. I fasted frequently because they said we had to understand the suffering Jesus went through for us.'

Cope-Faulkner blacked out and came to on a train on her way to see her parents, to whom she eventually told everything. She saw a psychiatrist for three years and was put on antidepressants, and with help from cult experts she learned that she had been mind-controlled. 'I still find it hard to trust people, and I can't get close to anyone,' she confesses.

At least 34 campuses have banned cults from their premises,

How cults recruit
(according to the Cult Information Centre)

- Chanting and singing: eliminating non-cult ideas through group repetition of mind-narrowing chants and phrases
- Confession: encouraging the destruction of individual ego through confession of personal weaknesses and innermost feelings or doubts
- Isolation: inducing loss of reality by physical separation from family, friends and normal society
- Controlled approval: maintaining vulnerability and confusion by alternately rewarding and punishing similar actions
- Change of diet: creating disorientation and increased susceptibility to emotional arousal by depriving the nervous system of nutrients through diets or fasting
- Sleep deprivation and fatigue, creating disorientation and vulnerability
- Removal of privacy: achieving loss of ability to evaluate logically by preventing private contemplation
- 'Love-bombing': creating a sense of family and belonging through hugging, kissing, touching and flattery
- Hypnosis: inducing high suggestibility by hypnosis, often thinly disguised as relaxation or meditation
- Peer-group pressure: suppressing doubt and resistance to new ideas by exploiting the need to belong
- Rejection of old values: accelerating acceptance of new lifestyle by constantly denouncing former values and beliefs

but somehow these groups still manage to recruit students, either by wandering in and chatting to people or by recruiting in town centres around the universities. Verity Coyle, vice-president of welfare for the National Union of Students, says, 'Cults recruit in a sly way, and it's all about misinformation. We've had radical Islamic groups recruiting here where police have been called, and there has been a definite rise in pseudo-Christian groups, like the group formerly known as International Churches of Christ, who prey on vulnerable people. These cults are very good at distributing information, but universities don't always like to publicise the fact that they have a cult problem.'

When a student sets up a group at university, which many do during an organised 'Societies Week', they must create a constitution, and any sexuality, race or gender issues that run against the grain of equality legislation will prevent the group being formed. Most cults, however, are more insidious and recruiters are trained to recognise a good target whom they will court off campus.

It's only when a student leaves a cult that any warnings about cult activity may spread through university populations, but this happens rarely as the person is usually too traumatised to remain around other members and will often switch to another university or drop out altogether.

Jeannie Mills, former member of the People's Temple, famously said: 'When you meet the friendliest people you have ever known, who introduce you to the most loving group of people you have ever encountered, and you find the leader to be the most inspired, caring, compassionate and understanding person you've ever met, and then you learn that the cause of the group is something you never dared hope could be accomplished, and all of this sounds too good to be true – it probably is too good to be true! Don't give up on your education, your hopes and ambitions to follow a rainbow.' After Mills left the group, she was found murdered.

- For a copy of the booklet *Cults: A Practical Guide*, contact the Cult Information Centre, BCM Cults, London WC1N 3XX or telephone 0870 777 3800. Or visit their website: www.cultinformation.org.uk

Religious tolerance and intolerance

Overview; definitions of terms

Overview

Most people agree that:

■ Racism means the expression of hatred towards, or the desire to discriminate against, persons of a specific race, usually a minority.

■ Sexism means the expression of hatred towards, or the desire to discriminate against, persons of a specific gender, usually female or intersexual.

■ Homophobia now means the expression of hatred towards, or the desire to discriminate against, persons of a specific sexual orientation, usually homosexual or bisexual. (It used to mean fear of homosexuals; some still hold to this definition.)

We feel that the English language needs a new word. We suggest:

■ Relism, meaning 'the expression of hatred towards, or discrimination against, persons of a specific religion affiliation, usually a minority faith'.

Unfortunately, this word does not exist, yet. We have to use phrases such as: 'religious intolerance' and 'religious tolerance'. And these have many conflicting meanings to various individuals and groups.

In this article the meaning of the term 'religious tolerance' does not involve:

■ Believing that all religions are the same. In fact, religions differ greatly in their beliefs and practices. So do divisions within a given religion.

■ Believing that all sets of religious beliefs are equally true. Many people consider their beliefs to be true and others to be at least partly false.

■ Believing that all faiths are

By B.A. Robinson

equally beneficial and equally harmless to society. In our opinion, some religions are less beneficial to society because they teach hatred, racism, sexism, homophobia, etc.

■ Believing that all religious groups are equally beneficial and equally harmless to their followers. Some religions expect their members to follow practices that are hazardous to their health, and shorten their lives.

■ Refraining from criticising religious practices of others. Some religions teach their followers to actively discriminate on the basis of race, gender, sexual orientation, nationality, etc. Such practices, in our opinion, should be freely criticised.

■ Refraining from talking about your beliefs to others. One should

feel free to discuss beliefs of all types. Of course, if the other person indicates that they don't want to talk about religion, then continued proselytising is a form of harassment.

■ Ignoring your own religious ideas. It is not necessary, nor is it desirable, for an individual to suppress their own religious beliefs, in order to accept the right of another person to follow a different religion. It is not necessary to accept others' beliefs as valid. A tolerant person merely extends to all people a fundamental human right: freedom of religious belief.

In this article the meaning of the term 'religious tolerance' does involve:

■ Accepting that followers of various religions consider their own beliefs to be true. Most people believe that their religious beliefs are true, perhaps even true on an absolute scale.

- Allowing others to hold religious beliefs that are different from yours. No society is truly free unless there is freedom of religious association, speech and belief for all.
- Allowing others to freely change their religion, or denomination or beliefs. Freedom of religion includes the right to change one's faith.
- Allowing others to practise their religious faith, within reasonable limits. Religion is more than belief; it involves practices as well.
- Refusing to discriminate in employment, accommodation etc. on religious grounds. People who follow minority religions have the right to be treated fairly in the workplace and society generally.
- Making a reasonable effort to accommodate other people's religious needs. For example:
  – Allowing an employee to work overtime in order to take off a religious festival or holy day that is significant to them.
  – Scheduling meetings so that they do not conflict with common holy days.

You, of course, may wish to define religious tolerance differently.

Various definitions of 'Religious tolerance'

We have searched through a number of American and British dictionaries. We particularly like *The Concise Oxford Dictionary*'s (1960) definition of toleration. It says, in part:
- 'recognition of right of private judgment in religious matters,
- liberty to uphold one's religious opinions and forms of worship, or
- to enjoy all social privileges etc. without regard to religious differences.'

This definition views religious toleration as a human rights issue. A person is tolerant when they respect the right of others to hold different religious beliefs. A person might believe that their own faith is the only valid religion – the one fully approved of and created by God. They might consider all other religions as profoundly evil. Yet, they can still be religiously tolerant towards others if they recognise that all individuals and religious groups have the basic human right of religious liberty – to freely follow their faith's beliefs and practices.

An excellent definition of 'religious tolerance' is published on 'Apologetics Index', an Evangelical Christian counter-cult website.

Webmaster Anton Hein defines it as: 'Acknowledging and supporting that individuals have the right and freedom to their own beliefs and related legitimate practices, without necessarily validating those beliefs or practices.'[1]

We are religiously tolerant when we give others the freedom to do things and believe things, even though we feel that they are wrong! To some people, this is not easy. Some feel that their religion is the only true faith, and that to oppress followers of another religion is to promote God's will in society. We support their right to believe this. But we oppose them if they want to take action to oppress others. That path leads to the killing fields of Bosnia-Herzegovina, massacres in East Timor, the gas chambers of Nazi Germany and numerous other horrors.

Reference:
1. Anton Hein, 'Religious Freedom, Tolerance, and Intolerance,' at: http://www.gospelcom.net/

- The above information is from Ontario Consultants on Religious Tolerance's website which can be found at www.religioustolerance.org

A guide to new anti-discrimination legislation

The Employment Equality (Religion or Belief) Regulations 2003 came into force on 2 December 2003. These make it unlawful to discriminate on the grounds of religion or belief in employment and vocational training. The legislation is required to comply with the EC Equal Treatment Framework Directive.

By Colin Cottell

What is covered
Simon Steen of Steen & Co, employment solicitors in Oxford, says: 'The regulations will prohibit direct discrimination, indirect discrimination, victimisation and harassment. They will cover all stages of the employment relationship including recruitment, promotion, the terms and conditions of employment and dismissal.'

How is religion or belief defined?
The term 'religion or belief' is defined in the regulations as 'any religion, religious belief, or similar philosophical belief'. But according to Mr Steen: 'It does not include philosophical or political beliefs unless they are similar to a religious belief.' So single issue campaigners such as anti-abortion campaigners will not be covered, he says.

While Christians, Muslims and Jews will clearly be covered, defining what constitutes a religion or a belief is a grey area. Are Druids, Pagans and Rastafarians included, for example? Some employment lawyers believe they are. The Department of Trade and Industry (DTI) has issued guidance but the courts will have to decide on a case-by-case basis, says Mr Steen. The regulations also cover those who have no belief.

Exceptions

The main exception to the regulations is discrimination where there is a genuine occupational requirement (GOR) that the holder of the job is of a particular religious belief. 'For example, the job of a teacher in a religious school would most probably be considered a post where discrimination should be allowed,' says Mr Steen. Churches, and other organisations based on a religious or belief ethos may also be successful in applying for a GOR.

Penalties

An employer will be liable for the unlawful actions of its employees. This is the case whether or not it knew or approved of those acts. There is no limit on levels of awards against employers.

However, individual employees could be personally liable and ordered to pay compensation to the victim. This is more likely where employers are able to successfully argue that they took reasonable steps to prevent employees from behaving unlawfully – for example, ensuring all staff attended equality training.

What should you do if you think you have suffered discrimination or harassment?

First make it clear to the person who is harassing you that their behaviour is unwelcome and that you want it to stop, advises the Advisory Conciliation and Arbitration Service (Acas). If that does not work take it up with your manager. Use your organisation's grievance procedure. Seek advice from your trade union.

If you are still not satisfied you may be able to make a complaint to an Employment Tribunal. Complaints must normally be brought within three months of the act you are complaining about.

An employee can in addition serve a questionnaire on their employer requesting further information, says Mr Steen. This may be admissible as evidence in any subsequent tribunal proceedings.

Actions for employers

The regulations do not require employers to provide time and facilities for religious or belief

The UK population by religion

	England and Wales	Scotland	Northern Ireland	Total UK	%
Christian	37,338,486	3,294,545	1,446,386	42,079,417	71.6
Buddhist	144,453	6,830	533	151,816	0.3
Hindu	552,421	5,564	825	558,810	1.0
Jewish	259,927	6,448	365	266,740	0.5
Muslim	1,546,626	42,557	1,943	1,591,126	2.7
Sikh	329,358	6,572	219	336,149	0.6
Other religion	150,720	26,974	1,143	178,837	0.3
All religions	40,321,991	3,389,490	1,451,414	45,162,895	76.8
No religion	7,709,267	1,394,460	45,909	n/a	15.5
Not stated	4,010,658	278,061	187,944	n/a	7.3
All no religion/not stated	11,719,925	1,672,521	233,853	13,626,299	23.2
Totals	**52,041,916**	**5,062,011**	**1,685,267**	**58,789,194**	**100**

Source: Office of National Statistics, Census 2001

observance in the workplace. However, according to Acas they should consider whether their policies, rules and procedures indirectly discriminate against workers of particular religions and if so whether reasonable changes might be made.

Definitions from the Acas guidelines

Direct discrimination
Treating someone less favourably on the grounds of their religion or belief. Example: a person is turned down for a job simply because he is a Hindu.

Indirect discrimination
Applying a criterion, provision or practice which disadvantages people of a particular religion or belief. Example: a no-headgear policy applied to all staff disadvantages Sikh staff who wear turbans for religious reasons.

Direct discrimination means treating someone less favourably on the grounds of their religion or belief. Example: a person is turned down for a job simply because he is a Hindu

---

Indirect discrimination is not always unlawful. However, for it to be justified an employer would have to show there was a real business need and that there was no alternative.

Harassment
Subjecting someone to unwanted conduct that violates a person's dignity or creates an intimidating, hostile, degrading, humiliating or offensive environment. Example: someone is constantly teased because of his or her beliefs.

A tribunal will take into account the perceptions of the person allegedly discriminated against. However, it will also test whether the action 'should reasonably be considered as having that effect'.

Victimisation
Victimising someone who has or intends to seek recourse under the regulations or someone who has or intends to give evidence in relation to a complaint of discrimination. Example: denying someone promotion because they supported an employee who took that employer to an Employment Tribunal on grounds of religious discrimination.

In certain circumstances discrimination or harassment could occur after the working relationship has ended. For example: a discriminatory job reference.

© Guardian Newspapers Limited 2004

The law on freedom of religion or belief

Information from the British Humanist Association

The Human Rights Act of 1998 incorporates into UK law the Council of Europe's Convention on Human Rights (ECHR), including its guarantee of freedom of religion or belief:

Article 9: Freedom of Thought, Conscience and Religion

1. Everyone has the right to freedom of thought, conscience and religion; this right includes freedom to change his religion or belief and freedom, either alone or in community with others and in public or private, to manifest his religion or belief, in worship, teaching, practice and observance.

2. Freedom to manifest one's religion or beliefs shall be subject only to such limitations as are prescribed by law and are necessary in a democratic society in the interests of public safety, for the protection of public order, health or morals, or for the protection of the rights and freedoms of others.

Article 9 of the ECHR has been tested in a number of court cases in Europe with the result that European law has moved in the direction of recognising a category of 'religion or belief', treated almost as a *single* category. These cases have shown beyond doubt that Article 9 embraces not only religious beliefs but also non-religious beliefs such as Humanism and atheism. Indeed, the first such case in the UK has recently been reported.

Thus we are able to base much of campaigning on firm Human Rights grounds, as shown by many items on our website.

This approach is reinforced by Article 14 of the ECHR which requires that Convention rights and freedoms 'be secured without discrimination on any ground' including religion etc, and section 6 of the Human Rights Act makes it 'unlawful for a public authority to act in a way which is incompatible with a Convention right'. Moreover, section 3 of the Human Rights Act declares:

'So far as it is possible to do so, primary legislation and subordinate legislation must be read and given effect in a way that is compatible with the Convention rights.'

The phrase 'religion or belief' is also used in Article 18 of the International Covenant on Civil and Political Rights:

'Everyone shall have the right to freedom of thought, conscience and religion. This right shall include freedom to have or adopt a religion or belief of his choice, and freedom, either individually or in community with others and in public or private, to manifest his religion or belief in worship, observance, practice or teaching.'

This was glossed by the UN Human Rights Committee:

'Article 18 protects theistic, non-theistic and atheistic beliefs, as well as the right not to profess any religion or belief. The terms belief and religion are to be broadly construed.

Article 18 is not limited in its application to traditional religions or to religions and beliefs with institutional characteristics or practices analogous to those of traditional religions.' General comment 22 (30/07/93)

The phrase has also been adopted in the European Union directive on religious and other discrimination in employment:

'The purpose of this Directive is to lay down a general framework for combating discrimination on the grounds of religion or belief, disability, age or sexual orientation as regards employment and occupation, with a view to putting into effect in the Member States the principle of equal treatment.'

Council directive 2000/78/EC of 27 November 2000 and hence in the new Employment Equality (Religion or Belief) Regulations 2003.

■ The above information is from the British Humanist Association's website which can be found at www.humanism.org.uk

© British Humanist Association

Teaching tolerance

We should abolish faith schools – they breed only intolerance and isolation

The London School of Islamics claimed last week that the 16-year-old Muslim girl murdered by her father in an 'honour killing' was really the victim of British state education. 'The tragedy could have been avoided if the poor girl was educated in a Muslim school by Muslim teachers,' it says. Muslims should not have to 'send their children to state schools where they are exposed to teachers who have no respect for Islamic faith and Muslim community'.

The solution, predictably, is more faith schools. These eliminate the behaviour in daughters which leads fathers to kill them.

Islam is not the only faith to have seen 'honour killings'. Scotland Yard believes there were 12 in Britain last year, and that they also occur in Sikh and Christian families. It is not the only religion to demand the right to educate its children away from the contaminating influence of those of other faiths or none. Britain has nearly 5,000 Church of England state schools, more than 2,000 Roman Catholic schools, and a sprinkling of Jewish, Muslim and Sikh schools.

The School of Islamics does not condone honour killings. It says they are 'un-Islamic', just as a Christian might say they were 'un-Christian' and talk of 'Christian values'. There isn't a more mischievous phrase in the language. It's a way of colonising values such as truthfulness and kindness, and implying that non-Christians cannot share them.

At the orthodox Jewish school near my home, the playground jokes are often racist ones, mostly about Arab Muslims. At the Catholic school where I was educated, we were especially contemptuous of the Church of England, whose minions, we were taught, had tortured and executed our martyrs under Elizabeth I. We were not taught that, during the previous reign, our priests had done the torturing.

By Francis Beckett

When Protestants in Northern Ireland stoned small children as they walked to their Catholic school, they were partly reflecting a society where most people went to faith schools and learned to despise each other. The religious zealotry that fuels conflicts all over the world, from Northern Ireland to the Middle East, is nurtured in faith schools, even though their teachers often try hard to inculcate tolerance.

> ### Far from wanting more faith schools in the state system, we should abolish the ones we have, turning them into schools that welcome those of all faiths and none

The better alternative is the comprehensive school my daughter attends, whose intake reflects the rich cultural mix of north London. She might find herself sitting beside a Muslim in one lesson, a Sikh in the next, a Catholic in the next. She will grow up understanding and respecting all faiths – except, perhaps, one. Though orthodox Jews form a strong faith community where I live, none of them are at my daughter's school. They are segregated in the faith school down the road, where they mix only with other orthodox Jews.

Far from wanting more faith schools in the state system, we should abolish the ones we have, turning them into schools that welcome those of all faiths and none. But for the moment, it isn't going to happen, because many faith schools get good examination results. They get them, not by being especially good schools, but by selecting their pupils in ways that are not open to other schools.

In order to get their son into the London Oratory, Tony and Cherie Blair had to present themselves and him before the headteacher. He interviews candidates, according to the prospectus, in order to 'assess Catholicity, practice and commitment and whether the aims, attitudes, values and expectations of the parents and the boy are in harmony with those of the school'. He also assesses 'commitment to the ethos of the London Oratory school, to the Church and to Catholic education'. He takes bright pupils from motivated families, who are likely to do well.

The bottom line is that parents have to be of the faith. So ordinarily truthful people, as their child reaches the age of 11, get religion all of a sudden. You see them hanging round the local church or synagogue, pathetically trying to look as though they've been there every week of their lives.

So, on the debit side, faith schools turn communities against each other, and turn honest people into liars. On the credit side, they teach girls behaviour that makes it less likely their fathers will slit their throats. Surely it would be better to hound the fathers than for the state to provide the education ghettoes in which these fathers like to immure their children?

But if we must have faith schools, let us be fair about it.

Atheists and humanists can live good lives just as much as Christians or Muslims – better, in fact, because we don't expect heavenly reward. Our kindness is not a spiritual get-rich-quick policy, nor our truthfulness a means of piling up celestial stock options.

A recent British Humanist Association survey showed that, for many families, the only nearby state school available is a faith school. These families get no help or sympathy from the state – unlike religious families, whom the authorities work hard to satisfy, even paying their fares to distant faith schools.

If there are to be state schools for faith communities, what about one for mine? We godless ones probably represent the fastest-growing faith community in Britain. Yet there has been no move to set up faith schools that will teach 'humanist values' and point out to fathers that killing their daughters is 'un-humanist'. It's about time there was.

■ This article first appeared in *The Guardian*, 10 October 2003.
© *Francis Beckett*

Anger over call to teach children atheism in school

A report urging the teaching of atheism in school as part of religious education was condemned by critics 15 February 2004 as a 'betrayal of children' and 'quite wrong'.

Lessons should be renamed religious, philosophical and moral education and teach different 'belief systems' such as agnosticism and humanism, according to the Institute for Public Policy Research.

The left-of-centre think tank's report, published 16 February 2004, prompted a mixed response. The Church of England and Muslim Council of Britain were largely unconcerned saying that atheism had always been discussed during RE lessons.

But the Campaign for Real Education said the teaching of non-religious beliefs would 'deny children their Christian heritage'. Canon John Hall, the Church of England's chief education officer, said: 'It is very important that other faiths are taught as well [as Christianity] because we need to respect and take into account other world views.

By Nicola Woolcock

'It's entirely appropriate that religious education recognises that some people do not believe in God.'

Tahir Alam, chairman of the Muslim Council of Britain's education committee, said atheism was already discussed in religious lessons.

'It's a reflection of our society,' he said. 'The question we should ask is how religion is taught and how much time is spent discussing atheism.'

But a spokesman for the CRE attacked the report, saying: 'Atheism

'It is important we learn both to converse with people of different faiths and think critically about our own'

is not a religion. To change religious education into spiritual education would be quite wrong. We would deny children their Christian heritage. RE lessons should be about the teachings of Christianity, and possibly other religions, but not secular beliefs.

'It's straying down the road of philosophy.'

Ann Widdecombe, the Conservative MP who converted to Catholicism, said: 'It's a betrayal of children.'

Ben Rogers, author of the IPPR report, said: 'It is important we learn both to converse with people of different faiths and think critically about our own.'

Religious education is a compulsory subject in English and Welsh schools but is not part of the national curriculum.

A Department for Education and Skills spokesman said: 'Non-religious belief systems have been taught in schools for years alongside the study of the main religious beliefs.'
© *Telegraph Group Limited, London 2004*

BHA warns on 'incitement to religious hatred'

BHA urges caution on 'religious hatred'

Humanists support the call for a law on incitement to religious hatred – but not the one that Blunkett wants.

The British Humanist Association (BHA) welcomes David Blunkett's announcement that the Government intends to introduce an offence of incitement to religious hatred as soon as possible to help tackle extremists who use religion to stir up hatred in society – but warns that legislation will have to be very carefully framed in order to protect freedom of speech, and that it must also protect the non-religious.

'The Government has a clear responsibility to protect its citizens from incitement to hatred, whether on grounds of race, religion, sexuality or any such reason,' said Hanne Stinson, the BHA's Executive Director, 'but in the case of religion, it is essential that any such law focuses exclusively on protection against incitement of hatred of people, without imposing unacceptable restrictions on legitimate criticism of beliefs and practices. It must also protect people with non-religious beliefs as well as the religious.'

'In 2003, the Lords Select Committee on Religious Offences heard compelling evidence that racists have been so inhibited by the law on incitement of racial hatred that they have cynically switched to inciting hatred against Asians as Muslims rather than on race grounds and have thus avoided prosecution, so there is a clear need for legislation. But the new legislation must not be based on the model of the race hate law (i.e. on the Public Order Act model) which would restrict free speech. The problem with the Public Order Act model is that it puts the emphasis on the words used, rather than their context or likely effect, and there is no doubt that in some cases the words used in, say, a serious article on public

BRITISH HUMANIST ASSOCIATION
for the one life we have

policy, could incite hatred if shouted on a street corner in an area where feelings are already running high,' she said.

When the House of Lords debated the Select Committee report in 2004 the British Muslim Research Council, Justice and the British Humanist Association jointly issued a briefing proposing an alternative formulation for legislation on incitement to hatred on grounds of religion or belief – the same formulation that was originally suggested by the BHA in a submission to the Select Committee. The BHA formulation focuses on the effect and/or intention of the offender, and therefore avoids the serious risks to freedom of speech of the Public Order Act model.

'There are many things that can be legitimately criticised in religion,' said Hanne Stinson . 'The differences between race and religion are many and profound: religions make extensive and often mutually incompatible claims about the nature of life and the world – claims that can legitimately be appraised and argued over. There is no parallel for race. And religions, unlike race, set out to dictate their followers' attitudes and behaviour, sometimes in ways that are extremely controversial. The religions also exert influence on social attitudes and national and international policy – it has to be legitimate to criticise.'

Notes:
David Blunkett made his new proposals on 'incitement to religious hatred' as part of a wide-ranging speech on 'New challenges for race equality and community cohesion in the 21st century' at an ippr event on 7 July 2004. Full speech at http://www.homeoffice.gov.uk/docs3/race-speech.pdf

The BHA's proposed formulation for a law on incitement to hatred on grounds of religion or belief, endorsed by the British Muslim Research Council and Justice, is:

1. It is an offence for a person publicly to use words or behaviour or to display any material:
a) by which he incites or intends to incite hatred against persons based on their membership (or presumed membership) of a religious group, or
b) in such manner and circumstances that a reasonable person would think that such hatred is likely to be stirred up.

2. For the purpose of section 1:
a) 'religious group' means a group defined by reference to religion or belief or the absence of any, or any particular, religion or belief
b) 'presumed' means presumed by the offender
c) 'membership' in relation to a religious group includes association with members of that group.

The law on incitement to racial hatred in Part III of the Public Order Act 1986 is based on the use of 'threatening or abusive or insulting words or behaviour'.

■ The above information is from the British Humanist Association's website which can be found at www.humanism.org.uk
© British Humanist Association

British hostility to Muslims 'could trigger riots'

By Jamie Doward and Gaby Hinsliff

Hostility towards Islam permeates every part of British society and will spark race riots unless urgent action is taken to integrate Muslim youths into society, according to a devastating report.

The Commission on British Muslims and Islamophobia (CBMI), which is chaired by a key government adviser to the Stephen Lawrence inquiry, warns that more and more Muslims feel excluded from society and simmering tensions, especially in northern English towns, are in danger of boiling over.

Members of the commission interviewed scores of British Muslims for their report, which was published in July 2004 and will conclude that Britain is 'institutionally Islamophobic'.

It emerged 22 July 2004, that the government is considering new laws to stop radical Muslim clerics coming from overseas to preach in Britain. According to reports in a Sunday newspaper imams will have to pass a 'civic engagement test' which will include an English language exam and questions on British culture. Public funds will be provided for the training of home-grown clerics in order to halt the influx of militant preachers from the Middle East.

The report produces a raft of evidence suggesting that since the 11 September attacks there has been a sharp rise in attacks on followers of Islam and their mosques and a rise in anti-Muslim sentiment across a range of UK institutions. Ahmed Versi, editor of the *Muslim News*, who gave evidence, said: 'We have reported cases of mosques being firebombed, paint being thrown at mosques, mosques being covered in graffiti, threats made, women being spat upon, eggs being thrown. It is the visible symbols of Islam that are being attacked.'

Dr Richard Stone, chair of the commission and an adviser to Sir

William Macpherson's inquiry into the murder of Stephen Lawrence, warns in a foreword to the report that: 'There is now renewed talk of a clash of civilisations, a new global cold war, and mounting concern that the already fragile foothold gained by Muslim communities in Britain is threatened by ignorance and intolerance.'

> **'The perception that our government is pandering to the neoconservatives of America has given rise to the belief that all Muslims are implicated in the aggression'**

The report suggests the situation in Iraq has had a negative impact on religious tolerance in British society. It quotes from an interview with Labour peer Baroness Uddin, who comments that: 'The perception that our government is pandering to the neoconservatives of America has given rise to the belief that all Muslims are implicated in the aggression. Each of us is constantly being asked to apologise for acts of terror that befall the world.'

Sadiq Khan, chair of the Muslim Council of Britain's legal affairs committee, told the commission, which was launched by Jack Straw in 1997, that recent changes in the law had also played a part.

'Laws such as the Terrorism Act 2000 and the Anti-Terrorism Crime Security Act 2001 have helped to create a climate of fear,' he said. 'They have led to the internment in the UK of Muslim men, respectable charities having their funds seized, and charities suffering because Muslims are reluctant to donate for fear of being accused of funding "terrorists".'

More than 35,000 Muslims were stopped and searched last year, with fewer than 50 charged. Three years ago only around 2,000 Muslims were stopped and searched.

Asian peer Lord Ahmed, a leading critic of Muslim extremism, told *The Observer* he had twice been stopped and searched in recent months at Heathrow airport.

Statistics also show a sharp rise in the number of Muslims jailed. In 2001 there were 6,095 in UK prisons compared with 731 in 1991. Muslims comprise 9 per cent of the prison population but only 3 per cent of the population as whole.

'Islamophobia in Britain has become institutionalised. If we don't take positive action to embrace the young Muslim men in this country, we are going to have an urgent problem,' Stone said. 'We're going to have real anger and riots with young Muslims pitched against the police.'

The report is critical of the media's treatment of Islam, especially its coverage of Abu Hamza, the radical cleric who was arrested in July 2004.

■ This article first appeared in *The Observer*, 30 May 2004

© *Guardian Newspapers Limited 2004*

Religion as a fig leaf for racism

The BNP is now riding a broad wave of respectable Islamophobia

By Jeremy Seabrook

When a BBC reporter infiltrated the British National Party by posing as a football hooligan, he caught on camera several activists admitting to violent assaults on Asians and repeatedly putting excrement through the letterbox of an Asian family's home. Six of the people he secretly filmed were arrested in July 2004. This appears to confirm the effectiveness of this hard-hitting demolition of a party desperately seeking respectability.

But however clear its exposure of repellent beliefs and values, the documentary did not seek to address the reasons why 800,000 or so people voted for the BNP in the European elections. What has made so many people ready to support the myth-makers of Britishness under threat?

Part of the answer is obvious. Many of those unable to escape poor white communities have seen their status decline from working class to underclass in one generation. The devastation of the industrial base was scarcely less traumatic than its imposition upon a wasting peasantry 200 years ago; and those left behind are indeed victims of global forces over which they have no control. The hatred of the stranger appears to give substance to the existence of these forces: xenophobia readily sees enemies in fellow-victims. And far from having been crushed by the BBC programme, the BNP was permitted to achieve that rarest of political breakthroughs: it was able to express what many other people are thinking.

The Islamophobia embraced by the BNP as a surrogate for its formally disavowed racism is by no means confined to the wasted landscapes of former working-class communities. It is deeply rooted and widespread, as was revealed by the success of Ukip (just listen to Robert Kilroy-Silk

assert that 'Muslims everywhere behave with equal savagery').

Indeed, Islamophobia is the only form of prejudice to which the middle class can readily admit: a religion which is perceived as advocating repression of women and hatred of gays renders acceptable forms of prejudice that would be unthinkable if directed against any other social group.

Officially, all right-thinking people have forsworn racism, now believed to fester principally among the no-hopers on rough estates. But

Islamophobia is the half-open door through which it makes its triumphal re-entry into respectable society. In recent articles in the *Sunday Telegraph*, Will Cummins has urged the Conservative party to espouse a more aggressive stand against Islam. 'Do the Tories not sense the enormous popular groundswell against Islam? Charges of "racism" would inevitably be made, but they would never stick. It is the black heart of Islam, not the black face, to which millions object.'

Perhaps this accounts for the extraordinarily easy time *Newsnight*'s Gavin Esler gave Nick Griffin, the leader of the BNP, after the documentary was screened. Esler

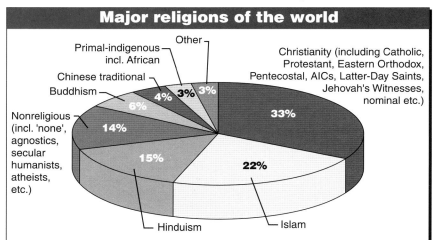

Major religions of the world

- Other
- Primal-indigenous incl. African
- Chinese traditional
- Buddhism
- Nonreligious (incl. 'none', agnostics, secular humanists, atheists, etc.)
- Christianity (including Catholic, Protestant, Eastern Orthodox, Pentecostal, AICs, Latter-Day Saints, Jehovah's Witnesses, nominal etc.)
- Hinduism
- Islam

3% 3% 4% 6% 14% 15% 22% 33%

Major religions of the world ranked by adherents

#	Religion	Adherents	#	Religion	Adherents
1.	Christianity:	2 billion	11.	Spiritism	14 million
2.	Islam:	1.3 billion	12.	Judaism:	14 million
3.	Hinduism:	900 million	13.	Baha'i:	6 million
4.	Secular/Nonreligious/ Agnostic/Atheist:	850 million	14.	Jainism:	4 million
			15.	Shinto:	4 million
5.	Buddhism:	360 million	16.	Cao Dai:	3 million
6.	Chinese traditional religion:	225 million	17.	Tenrikyo:	2.4 million
7.	Primal-indigenous:	150 million	18.	Neo-Paganism:	1 million
8.	Afircan Traditional & Diasporic:	95 million	19.	Unitarian-Universalism:	800,000
			20.	Rastafarianism:	700,000
9.	Sikhism:	23 million	21.	Scientology:	600,000
10.	Juche:	19 million	22.	Zoroastrianism	150,000

Sizes shown are *approximate estimates*, and are here mainly for the purpose of ordering the groups, not providing a definitive number. This list is sociological in perspective.

Source: 2004 www.adherents.com

appeared stupefied by Griffin. He failed to challenge him when he stated that one of the 'angry young men' in the documentary had been 'ethnically cleansed by elements of the young Muslim community'. Nor did he contest the demented assertion that Islam spread through 'the rape of non-Muslim women'. He let pass, too, remarks on 'the progressive Islamification of the west. The total destruction of our civilisation within the next few decades' – a conspiracy theory that is emerging out of the shadows of the far right into an increasingly turbid mainstream: a *Spectator*'s cover story in July 2004 was headlined 'The Muslims are Coming'.

David Blunkett's desire to protect people from the incitement of hatred on the basis of religious belief is a recognition that

Islamophobia has become a refuge for racists. As Griffin was quick to point out, even secular liberals increasingly define 'Britishness' in opposition to 'medieval' Islamic values. They feel comfortable condemning Muslims because Islam is a religion, an adventitious rather than an ineradicable attribute. Ignoring the shift in self-identification that has taken place in recent years, and the fact that the overwhelming majority of Muslims are non-white, liberals argue that being Muslim is quite unlike ethnicity because people are free to embrace religion or set it aside.

The threat we now face is not simply the brutal behaviour of a minority of poor white men, but the creeping acceptability of the view that Islam itself represents a retro-

grade and 'primitive' kind of faith, which 'we' in our wisdom have outgrown.

Secularism, which liberals are so proud of, is not the opposite of the archaic superstition which they attribute to Islam. If we want to compare civilisational flaws, we are looking for our own in the wrong place. These occur in a quite different arena from the repression of women and gays, and are located among the injuries of excess that we have come to regard as normal; and that includes the impoverishment visited upon millions of people who thought they were working class, and woke up one day to discover that they were only white trash after all.

■ Jeremy Seabrook's latest book is *A World Growing Old*.

Religious rights

New legislation will allow workers to take time off for spiritual observance. Roisin Woolnough looks at the details

Christians have long had it easy in terms of being able to combine work with religious observance. Sundays, Christmas, Easter – the important days in the Christian calendar are free for the majority to do as they will. Now it's time for employers to make more allowances for those of other faiths as well. From 2 December 2003, new legislation comes into effect in the UK which formalises and extends the rights of employees of any faith to take time off work for religious observance. It could be an entire day to celebrate the Muslim festival Eid, for example, or 10 minutes at particular times of the day to pray. Druids could even take time off to mark the summer solstice.

The Employment Equality (Religion or Belief) Regulations 2003 prohibit direct and indirect discrimination on the grounds of religion or belief. There is no express right for employees to take time off for religious purposes, as employers do not have to grant requests if they conflict with operational needs, but

employers do risk liability for direct discrimination if they refuse to grant leave because of the employee's religion or belief. They also risk charges of indirect discrimination if they have company rules or practices that are disadvantageous to employees of a particular religion or belief and which cannot be justified for other reasons.

The Employment Equality (Religion or Belief) Regulations 2003 prohibit direct and indirect discrimination on the grounds of religion or belief

---

A central part of the regulations is the broad definition of what constitutes a religion or belief. It naturally encompasses those who define themselves as Muslim, Protestant, Roman Catholic,

Jehovah's Witness, Mormon, Sikh, Rastafarian and members of other 'official' religions, but it also includes beliefs such as druidism, pacifism, veganism, Scientology, atheism and agnosticism.

What the regulations are saying, in effect, is that all deeply held beliefs need to be taken seriously and, wherever possible, work should not prevent people from practising what they believe in. 'It is very heavily value-laden and a key part of the legislation is that you and I can almost invent our own personalised belief system,' says Dianah Worman, adviser on diversity at the Chartered Institute of Personnel and Development. 'It's as wide-ranging as that and there is no way we could have a total list.'

According to Makbool Javaid, employment partner at law firm DLA, a religion or belief is something that has three essential components: collective worship, a clear belief system and a profound belief affecting a person's way of life or view of the world. Javaid does not anticipate many problems with the regulations, although he thinks a potential flashpoint area could be when an employer does not believe that a particular religion or belief is valid. This would, of course, be more of an issue with unconventional beliefs such as paganism or Satanism. 'Problems could arise in areas where employers take the view that a religion is not a religion but something else, such as a cult,' he says.

Worman agrees that this is the area most likely to cause problems, particularly if the line manager concerned practises a different religion. However, she points out that this should not influence how they handle the request for time off for worship. 'Employers have to respect the fact that it's legitimate to have a different belief, even if it conflicts with your own religion,' she says.

Many companies already have prayer rooms for employees, but from 2 December it will be vital that employers provide the necessary facilities for staff who need to pray at certain times during the day. Equally important is that the layout and upkeep of such rooms is carefully monitored.

'Certain religions would be offended by idols, so you don't want any religious symbols in the room,' explains Javaid. 'You need to have rules about use of the room. That way, there is less likelihood of employers getting it wrong and causing aggravation,' he adds. Some faiths do not allow both sexes to use the same room, so that needs to be taken into account, or it might be that the room needs to face a particular direction or that washing facilities are required.

Employers and HR departments need to think the regulations through and be proactive so that they are ready to deal with any requests. Best practice would require efforts like having an annual schedule of when religious festivals and events take place and disseminating it among line managers. The HR team at Birmingham City Council does exactly that. 'Each year we send out a schedule of all main religious festivals, events, etc. to all chief officers and departmental personnel

managers,' says Lucy Phillips, employment equality manager at the council. Employees are entitled to take up to four days of leave (from their annual leave entitlement) to observe a religious holiday. If this conflicts with the council's needs, Phillips says, they try to make recompense to the individuals concerned. 'If an employee, due to operational requirements, is unable to take leave on a specific date, then that working day is treated as a bank holiday and therefore paid at an enhanced rate,' she says.

Employers are not legally bound to grant every request for time off for religious observance, but they are required to consider requests and justify any negative responses. Javaid says the two key words are flexibility and sensitivity, as should be the case with any request for time off or altered hours. 'Say you have an Orthodox Jew who wants to leave early on Fridays,' he explains. 'Maybe they could work through lunch instead or adjust their working hours – for example, working an extra hour one day so as to leave early on the Friday.'

Employers are not legally bound to grant every request for time off for religious observance, but they are required to consider requests and justify any negative responses

---

Problems could arise if the time that the employee wants to take off conflicts with operational requirements. Take the case above: if the

employer genuinely needs that individual to stay until the end of normal working hours on a Friday, then it is reasonable to stipulate that as a necessity. Employers are entitled to refuse requests, as long as they can prove there is a valid reason for doing so. 'If the employer has a genuine business case, that is justification,' says Javaid. 'It is all about balancing the needs of employer and employee.'

Should an employee feel their request for time off has been rejected unreasonably, they should raise the issue with the appropriate persons. In the first instance, this would be the line manager. Most companies have grievance procedures which can be invoked. HR and diversity teams exist precisely to deal with these kind of issues, so employees should make full use of them. The same goes for trade unions and staff bodies. Employment tribunals should only be considered as a last resort, because they will not look kindly on complainants who have not exhausted all available internal channels first.

Even before this new legislation, the law found ways to protect those discriminated against on the basis of religion. A few years ago, an industrial tribunal ruled against a West Yorkshire textile firm that had disciplined Muslim employees for taking a day off for Eid. The company had announced that no staff could take a non-statutory holiday during its busiest months, even though this coincided with the Islamic festival. The company had, for the previous 20 years, allowed its Muslim employees the necessary leave – unpaid if they had already used up their annual paid allowance. If their absence caused any backlog, they worked additional hours until it was cleared. When 17 Muslims took time off for Eid anyway, the company disciplined them and issued final written warnings. The tribunal found that the Muslims had been unlawfully discriminated against on grounds of race, and awarded them each £1,000 in compensation.

While employment experts don't think the floodgates will open when the new regulations come into force, they think there will be a steady trickle of cases as awareness grows.

© *Guardian Newspapers Limited 2004*

A new threat to the rights of non-believers

Religious discrimination legislation

Summary

1. The National Secular Society wants to see a fair and just society in which no one is disadvantaged because of factors beyond their control. However, we would resist most strongly any attempt to give special privilege or protection to any religious or non-religious beliefs, sensibilities, groups or institutions.

2. We believe that any legislation must be framed in such a way that it does not open the door for endless litigation which will eventually result in religious believers gaining special privileges that are denied to others. This means that only individual believers should benefit from protective laws, not what they believe. We want to save people from being disadvantaged in housing, employment and the receipt of services, and we want to see them protected from violence, intimidation and harassment, but we do not wish to see any restrictions placed on the critical examination of their religion or its activities.

3. We want to ensure that other groups and minorities, such as non-believers and homosexuals, are not left unprotected and liable to suffer discrimination at the hands of the religious. Any legislation must include a clause that forbids religious people from using their faith as an excuse to disadvantage other people. One way to do this would be to introduce a more generalised Equalities Act that would cover all minorities that are disadvantaged. This would have the effect of not making religion a special case, and thereby avoiding the resentment and conflict that would inevitably arise from laws that only protect religion and the religious.

National Secular Society

4. We want to ensure that free speech is protected, and this means that nothing should be included in any legislation that would permit religious believers to silence reasonable or even vigorous criticism – so long as it does not incite hatred – on the grounds that their religious feelings or sensibilities have been hurt or outraged. In order to remove feelings of disadvantage, the blasphemy laws should be abolished completely, as recommended on two occasions by the Law Commission. The disadvantages and dangers of attempting to extend the blasphemy laws to cover other religions far outweigh any possible advantages.

5. Ultimately, there can be no religious equality in this country while the Church of England remains established by law. The rights and privileges that go with this status ensure that true equality and freedom from discrimination will remain impossible. The Government has shown little willingness to tackle the undoubtedly complex and controversial issue of disestablishment, although there has been some debate about it within the Church of England itself. In the long term, however, disestablishment of the Church of England is the only logical way forward.

6. But what comes after disestablishment? We feel that the answer to the growing resentment about the inequality of treatment meted out to religions in this country is to secularise our public life, and so ensure that all can be included and none can be privileged. This could be achieved by the following:

1. The Church of England should be disestablished and the Act of Settlement, that forbids the heir to the throne from marrying a Catholic, must be repealed.

2. The bishops should be removed from the House of Lords (and no other ex-officio religious Lords created).

3. The blasphemy laws should be abolished and not extended.

4. Religious schools should be removed from the state system and religious education should be non-denominational and multicultural in nature.

5. There should be no prayers or other acts of worship in parliament, council chambers or other places used by statutory bodies.

6. All religious oaths connected with public office should be replaced by affirmations.

7. All public money that is given to religious organisations for welfare purposes should be ring-fenced to ensure it is used entirely for the benefit of the service users and not for proselytisation. Any religious group in receipt of public funds must agree to embrace a nationally agreed equal opportunities policy.

8. No public money should be spent on religious observances or rituals. Grants to maintain places of worship should be restricted to listed buildings of historic importance. All other tax advantages and privileges enjoyed by religious organisations should be removed.

9. By embracing secularism in this way, everyone can be included, regardless of their religion or lack of it, and no one can obtain unfair advantage. Religious observance will be free and protected, but it will be separate from the state and a matter of private and personal significance only.

10. Religious believers should be protected from discrimination, but religious beliefs must be open to the same critical examination as any other ideas or beliefs.

■ The above information is from the National Secular Society's website: www.secularism.org.uk

© Reproduced by kind permission of the National Secular Society

Religious diversity

A humanist perspective

BRITISH **HUMANIST** ASSOCIATION
for the one life we have

Humanists are non-religious people who live by moral principles based on reason and respect for others, not unquestioning obedience to rules. Like the vast majority of people, they accept the scientific theory of evolution, which means that human beings are all members of the same species and share the same ancestors. We are all, in effect, distantly related to each other, so it is not surprising that we share many of the same feelings and needs, and have a great deal in common. We also evolved as social animals, which means that we live in large groups and have to learn to work and get on with each other. A few centuries ago people rarely moved far from home or met people with different world views; nowadays most of us live and work alongside people of many different nationalities, races, religions and beliefs. Humanists believe that, even though it can cause tensions, diversity enriches our lives. As the philosopher Karl Popper put it in *The Open Society and its Enemies* (1945), 'Rationalism is an attitude of readiness to listen to contrary arguments and to learn from experience' of admitting that 'I may be wrong and you may be right and, by an effort, we may get nearer the truth.'

We all have beliefs about life's 'ultimate questions' – for some these beliefs are religious and for others they are not. Both kinds of belief may be called world views, or life stances or philosophies. The Universal Declaration of Human Rights, the European Convention on Human Rights and the UK Human Rights Act recognise both religious and non-religious beliefs and guarantee freedom of religion and belief. Humanists strongly support human rights, which have been called 'values for a godless age'. Because humanists believe that we must try to make the only life we have as good as possible for everyone, they are committed to equality, democracy and a secular state which

> *We all have beliefs about life's 'ultimate questions' – for some these beliefs are religious and for others they are not*

treats all religions and beliefs, including Humanism, equally and does not discriminate on grounds of religion or belief.

Unfortunately discrimination and various religious privileges are still common in the UK. For example, the Church of England still has 26 seats in the House of Lords; worship that is 'wholly or mainly of a broadly Christian character' has to take place every day in all state schools; the Government is encouraging the expansion of faith-based schools and faith-based welfare schemes; and some religious representatives have privileged access to Government departments.

It can be difficult to draw the line between steps to protect the right to believe and practise a religion or belief, and religious privilege – and humanists will sometimes differ on where they draw that line. Humanist judgements will be made on ethical grounds – bearing in mind human rights and the consequences of any action – and sometimes on pragmatic grounds – accepting that difference and diversity are aspects of modern life which can be valuable and which ought to be accommodated wherever possible without harmful consequences, in the interests of social harmony and what the philosopher John Stuart Mill called 'experiments in living'.

For example, the British Humanist Association (BHA) supports legislation to outlaw incitement to religious hatred, though it defends the right to criticise religion and opposes blasphemy laws. It generally supports 'reasonable accommodation' of religious beliefs and practices in society and schools: for example, it does not oppose women voluntarily wearing the hijab, or teachers or young people in schools voluntarily taking part in worship. We would like to see all schools accommodating religious diversity so that children of all faiths and none can attend the same schools, learning with and from each other. The BHA opposes school or workplace discrimination on grounds of religion or belief, though it recognises that for some jobs a particular belief is a genuine requirement – for example a vicar needs to be a Christian, and the Executive Director of the BHA needs to be a humanist. We have also proposed more public holidays, some of which could be chosen by non-Christian religions.

However, humanists believe that 'accommodations' must be reasonable, that is, that they should not have damaging consequences such as harming children or discriminating against non-religious people, for example by expecting them to work longer or unsocial hours in order to permit religious colleagues to practise their beliefs. Many humanists are concerned about the cruelty to animals involved in ritual slaughter for kosher and halal meat, and believe that this should join other long-abandoned traditional practices now seen as incompatible with civilised humane life. Humanists do not think that religious reasons or traditions are enough to justify laws that restrict the freedoms of others, and worry that the access that some religious groups have to Government departments may give them disproportionate influence. Humanists would always support important rights and freedoms (such as children's welfare, sex equality, birth control, scientific research, and voluntary euthanasia) against attempts to limit or ban them on religious grounds.

■ The above information is from the British Humanist Association's website which can be found at www.humanism.org.uk

© British Humanist Association

Faith value

Information from the Salvation Army. By Nigel Bovey

Reports of God's death have been greatly exaggerated. Church attendance may be down and the distinctive nature of Sundays changed but more than three-quarters of the population still say they belong to a faith community.

In May 2004, the Home Office announced the results of its Citizenship Survey. The survey, carried out in 2001, sought to discover whether religion was relevant in the lives of people in England and Wales. Of those questioned, 78 per cent said they have a religious affiliation.

The largest number (74 per cent) described themselves as Christian, with Muslims (2 per cent) and Hindus (1 per cent) as the next largest groups.

When asked 'What says something important about you?' respondents ranked faith below family, work and education but higher than potentially-divisive issues such as social class, country of origin, ethnicity, skin colour and sexuality.

Religion is often blamed as the cause of interracial conflict and prejudice. But these findings suggest that having a faith helps people put contentious issues into perspective. God is bigger than nationality, ethnicity or sexuality.

The Government knows the value of people of faith. Faith communities constitute a significant part of the voluntary and -community sector

Having faith is a positive life choice. It gives a person a sense of belonging. It is part of what makes them them. It gives them a set of values on which to base behaviour and attitude. It motivates them to be society's givers rather than takers.

The Government knows the value of people of faith. Faith communities constitute a significant part of the voluntary and community sector. They care for elderly people. They run recovery programmes for those blighted by addiction. They house homeless people. They care for people with Aids. They nurse the dying. They feed the hungry. They give time and attention to awkward teenagers. They teach children.

Is faith relevant in postmodern, 'secular' society? Yes. It most definitely is.

■ The above information is from *War Cry*, 29 May 2004, the Salvation Army's publication. For more information, visit their website which can be found at www.salvationarmy.org.uk

© Salvation Army

- The UK has greater religious diversity than any other country in the European Union. This is a direct result of historical immigration patterns, particularly times when people from Commonwealth countries were encouraged to enter the country to fill labour shortages. (p. 3)

- Based on the 2001 Census figures for England and Wales the two countries are made up of . . .
  - 37,338,486 Christians
  - 1,546,626 Muslims
  - 552,421 Hindus
  - 329,358 Sikhs
  - 259,927 Jews
  - 144,453 Buddhists.

- Despite the sharp decline in churchgoing and the growth of secularism, 37.3 million described their religion as Christianity, according to the 2001 Census. (p. 5)

- Two-thirds of UK 18- to 24-year-olds say they have no religious affiliation, compared to just a quarter of pensioners. (p. 6)

- 48 per cent of UK residents claim to belong to a religion, compared to 86 per cent in the United States and 92 per cent in Italy. (p. 6)

- It's time for people of different faiths to speak up louder about all the good things connected with religion: about the ways that religions help people and about the benefits this brings to individuals and communities. (p. 8)

- On an average Sunday, just seven per cent of Britons find their way to church, and a few more to the mosque or temple on other days of the week. (p. 9)

- Pupils should not just learn about religion but learn from religion by being taught to 'reflect and evaluate their own and others' beliefs about world issues such as peace and conflict, wealth and poverty and the importance of the environment'. (p. 15)

- New Religious Movements (NRMs), alternative religions, sects or cults all have technical definitions in the literature of the social sciences. (p. 19)

- Among the better-known such movements frequently referred to as 'cults' in this more popular sense are the Unification Church (the 'Moonies'), the International Society for Krishna Consciousness (the Hare Krishna), Scientology, the Rajneesh movement and The Family (once known as the Children of God). (p. 19)

- The Cult Information Centre says that the numbers of cults recruiting from universities has almost certainly increased – they estimate that there are 500 cult movements active in the UK today. (p. 24)

- We feel that the English language needs a new word. We suggest: Relism, meaning 'the expression of hatred towards, or discrimination against, persons of a specific religion affiliation, usually a minority faith'. (p. 26)

- A person is tolerant when they respect the right of others to hold different religious beliefs. A person might believe that their own faith is the only valid religion – the one fully approved of and created by God. They might consider all other religions as profoundly evil. Yet, they can still be religiously tolerant towards others if they recognise that all individuals and religious groups have the basic human right of religious liberty – to freely follow their faith's beliefs and practices. (p. 27)

- The Employment Equality (Religion or Belief) Regulations 2003 came into force in December 2003. These make it unlawful to discriminate on the grounds of religion or belief in employment and vocational training. (p. 27)

- Far from wanting more faith schools in the state system, we should abolish the ones we have, turning them into schools that welcome those of all faiths and none.

- 'It's entirely appropriate that religious education recognises that some people do not believe in God.' (p. 31)

- The British Humanist Association (BHA) welcomes David Blunkett's announcement that the Government intends to introduce an offence of incitement to religious hatred as soon as possible to help tackle extremists who use religion to stir up hatred in society – but warns that legislation will have to be very carefully framed in order to protect freedom of speech, and that it must also protect the non-religious. (p. 32)

- Statistics also show a sharp rise in the number of Muslims jailed. In 2001 there were 6,095 in UK prisons compared with 731 in 1991. Muslims comprise 9 per cent of the prison population but only 3 per cent of the population as whole. (p. 33)

- We all have beliefs about life's 'ultimate questions' – for some these beliefs are religious and for others they are not. (p. 38)

- Religion is often blamed as the cause of interracial conflict and prejudice. But these findings suggest that having a faith helps people put contentious issues into perspective. God is bigger than nationality, ethnicity or sexuality. (p. 39)

ADDITIONAL RESOURCES

You might like to contact the following organisations for further information. Due to the increasing cost of postage, many organisations cannot respond to enquiries unless they receive a stamped, addressed envelope.

British Humanist Association (BHA)
1 Gower Street
London, WC1E 6HD
Tel: 020 7079 3580
Fax: 020 7079 3588
E-mail: info@humanism.org.uk
Website: www.humanism.org.uk
The British Humanist Association is the UK's leading organisation for people concerned with ethics and society, free from religious and supernatural dogma. It represents, supports and serves humanists in the United Kingdom and is a registered charity with more than fifty affiliated local groups. Publishes a wide range of free briefings including the issues of racism, discrimination and prejudice, abortion, euthanasia and surrogacy.

Common Purpose
28-42 Banner Street
London, EC1Y 8QE
Tel: 020 7608 8100
Fax: 020 7336 6844
Website:
www.commonpurpose.org.uk
Common Purpose is an independent educational organisation which runs programmes for leaders, providing them with information, competencies and networks to help them become better leaders and to improve the way society works.

Cult Information Centre (CIC)
BCM Cults
London, WC1N 3XX
Tel: 0870 777 3800
Website:
www.cultinformation.co.uk
CIC is an educational charity providing advice and information for victims of cults, their families and friends, researchers and the media. It was the first educational organisation focusing critical concern on the harmful methods of the cults to be granted charitable status in the United Kingdom.

INFORM
London School of Economics
Houghton Street
London
WC2A 2AE
Tel: 020 7955 7654
E-mail: inform@lse.ac.uk
Website: www.inform.ac
INFORM is an independent charity that was founded in 1988 by Professor Eileen Barker with the help of British Home Office funding and the support of the mainstream Churches. It is based at the London School of Economics.
The primary aim of INFORM is to help people through providing them with accurate, balanced, up-to-date information about new and/or alternative religious or spiritual movements.

The Inter Faith Network
8A Lower Grosvenor Place
London
SW1W 0EN
Tel: 020 7931 7766
Fax: 020 7931 7722
E-mail: ifnet@interfaith.org.uk
Website: www.interfaith.org.uk
The Inter Faith Network for the UK works to build good relations between the communities of all the major faiths in Britain: Baha'i; Buddhist; Christian; Hindu; Jain; Jewish; Muslim; Sikh; and Zoroastrian.

National Secular Society
25 Red Lion Square
London, WC1R 4RL
Tel: 020 7404 3126
Website: www.secularism.org.uk
The National Secular Society is the national campaigning arm of the secularist movement, it:
keeps a high profile in the press and on TV and radio; closely monitors parliamentary business; makes submissions on issues important to secularists; informs ministers and government departments.

The National Youth Agency (NYA)
19-23 Humberstone Road
Leicester, LE5 3GJ
Tel: 0116 242 7350
Fax: 0116 242 7471
E-mail: nya@nya.org.uk
E-mail:
youthinformation@nya.org.uk
Website: www.nya.org.uk
Website:
www.youthinformation.com
The National Youth Agency aims to advance youth work to promote young people's personal and social development, and their voice, influence and place in society.

Salvation Army
101 Newington Causeway
Elephant and Castle
London, SE1 6BN
Tel: 020 7367 4500
Fax: 020 7367 4711
E-mail:
schools@salvationarmy.org.uk
Website:
www.salvationarmy.org.uk
Carrys the Gospel to all peoples in every land; gives practical expression of Christianity without regard to class, creed or race.

YoungMinds
102-108 Clerkenwell Road
London, EC1M 5SA
Tel: 020 7336 8445
Fax: 020 7336 8446
E-mail:
enquiries@youngminds.org.uk
Website: www.youngminds.org.uk
YoungMinds is the national charity committed to improving the mental health of all children and young people. YoungMinds Parents' Information Service, leaflets, seminars, consultancy and *YoungMinds* Magazine help young people, parents and professionals to understand when a young person is troubled and where to find help.

INDEX

ACKNOWLEDGEMENTS

The publisher is grateful for permission to reproduce the following material.

While every care has been taken to trace and acknowledge copyright, the publisher tenders its apology for any accidental infringement or where copyright has proved untraceable. The publisher would be pleased to come to a suitable arrangement in any such case with the rightful owner.

Chapter One: Religious Diversity

Guide to religions in the UK, © Guardian Newspapers Limited 2004, *Religions*, © Common Purpose 2004, *Census proves the force of Christianity*, © Telegraph Group Limited, London 2004, *Ethnicity and identity*, © Crown copyright is reproduced with the permission of Her Majesty's Stationery Office, *Turning from God*, © YoungMinds, *Belief*, © MORI, *Different faiths shared values*, © The Inter Faith Network, *We need to teach religion*, © Telegraph Group Limited, London 2004, *Food rules and religion*, © National Youth Agency, *The golden rule*, © British Humanist Association, *Wise and wonderful?*, © Guardian Newspapers Limited 2004, *Humanism becomes one of the new gods of RE*, © Telegraph Group Limited, London 2004, *What we believe in now*, © MORI, *Should faith-based projects try to promote their beliefs?*, © Young People Now, *Lure of the celebrity sect*, © Guardian Newspapers Limited 2004, *New religious movements*, © INFORM, *What is a cult?*, © Cult Information Centre, *Let us prey*, © Guardian Newspapers Limited 2004.

Chapter Two: Religious Tolerance

Religious tolerance and intolerance, © Ontario Consultants on Religious Tolerance (OCRT), *A guide to new anti-discrimination legislation*, © Guardian Newspapers Limited 2004, *The law on freedom of religion or belief*, © British Humanist Association, *Teaching tolerance*, © Francis Beckett, *Anger over call to teach children atheism in school*, © Telegraph Group Limited, London 2004, *BHA warns on 'incitement to religious hatred'*, © British Humanist Association, *British hostility to Muslims 'could trigger riots'*, © Guardian Newspapers Limited 2004, *Religion as a fig leaf for racism*, © Guardian Newspapers Limited 2004, *Major religions of the world*, © 2004 www.adherents.com, *Religious rights*, © Guardian Newspapers Limited 2004, *A new threat to the rights of non-believers*, © National Secular Society, *Religious diversity*, © British Humanist Association, *Faith value*, © Salvation Army.

Photographs and illustrations:

Pages 1, 24: Pumpkin House; pages 3, 11, 17: Angelo Madrid; pages 4, 14, 29, 37: Simon Kneebone; pages 8, 26: Bev Aisbett; pages 12, 23, 30: Don Hatcher.

Craig Donnellan
Cambridge
January, 2005